Education at SAGE

SAGE is a leading international publisher of journals, books, and electronic media for academic, educational, and professional markets.

Our education publishing includes:

- accessible and comprehensive texts for aspiring education professionals and practitioners looking to further their careers through continuing professional development

- inspirational advice and guidance for the classroom

- authoritative state of the art reference from the leading authors in the field

Find out more at: **www.sagepub.co.uk/education**

THE SCHOOL LEADER'S TOOLKIT

Practical Strategies for Leading and Managing

Edited by
MARY DAWE

Los Angeles | London | New Delhi
Singapore | Washington DC

Los Angeles | London | New Delhi
Singapore | Washington DC

SAGE Publications Ltd
1 Oliver's Yard
55 City Road
London EC1Y 1SP

SAGE Publications Inc.
2455 Teller Road
Thousand Oaks, California 91320

SAGE Publications India Pvt Ltd
B 1/I 1 Mohan Cooperative Industrial Area
Mathura Road
New Delhi 110 044

SAGE Publications Asia-Pacific Pte Ltd
3 Church Street
#10-04 Samsung Hub
Singapore 049483

Editor: Marianne Lagrange
Editorial assistant: Kathryn Bromwich
Production editor: Thea Watson
Copyeditor: Sharon Cawood
Proofreader: Gary Lister
Marketing manager: Lorna Patkai
Cover design: Wendy Scott
Typeset by: C&M Digitals (P) Ltd, Chennai, India
Printed in India by Replika Press Pvt Ltd

First published 2013

Library of Congress Control Number: 2011945293

British Library Cataloguing in Publication data

A catalogue record for this book is available from the British Library

ISBN 978-1-4462-0191-6
ISBN 978-1-4462-0192-3 (pbk)

Contents

Notes on Contributors   vi

Part I   Leading and Managing the School Workforce   **1**

1   Leading and Managing People, Mary Dawe   3

2   Wellbeing in Educational Settings, Domini Bingham   17

3   Conflict Resolution, Linda Trapnell   34

4   Leading Professional Learning and Development, Carol Taylor   44

5   Leading Support Staff, Pauline Lyons   62

Part II   Leading and Managing within the School   **77**

6   Leading and Managing Finance, Douglas MacIldowie   79

7   Managing Data, Jenny Francis   95

8   Leading the Curriculum, Tom Cragg   111

9   Leading and Managing Change, Sue Hellman   126

10   Leading and Managing in an Inclusive Environment, Louise Ishani with Elvira Gregory and Karla Martin   141

11   Using Teacher-Led Research for School Improvement, Kim Insley   161

Part III   Looking Outwards   **173**

12   Preparing for Ofsted, Barbara and Graham Saltmarsh   175

13   Creating Effective Networks, Caroline Dargan   189

Index   203

Notes on Contributors

Domini Bingham

Domini Bingham's background is in marketing and public relations, both in the public and private sectors and in international development, having worked for several years at the Commonwealth Secretariat. She is a tutor at the London Centre for Leadership in Learning at the Institute of Education (IoE) and a qualified teacher to adults and is passionate about adults achieving their potential and about addressing obstacles to achieving that. She has an MA in Lifelong Learning and is currently studying for her doctorate at the IoE, with research interests in leading for workplace, wellbeing and interculturalism.

Tom Cragg

Tom Cragg began his teaching career in 1999 in a Catholic comprehensive school in west London. He was head of a successful Modern Foreign Languages (MFL) department for six years, and performed the role of Gifted & Talented Coordinator for three years. He is now Assistant Principal at Chelsea Academy, where he is currently responsible for CPD, the Key Stage 4 curriculum and performance management.

Caroline Dargan

After several headships and leadership development roles, Caroline is now a consultant coach working with senior and middle leaders in the public/private sector. She is the Director of Dargan Associates, a client-centred facilitation company, which works with small and medium-sized groups in the private and public sectors. A qualified coach and highly experienced facilitator and mediator, she coaches teams through the organisational change management process and in leadership skill development.

Mary Dawe

Mary Dawe has over 30 years of experience in secondary education, including senior leadership. She played a principal role in developing Surrey's induction portfolio for newly qualified teachers, a training programme for NQTs and a programme for overseas trained teachers. She also worked with the TTA to develop the Career Entry Profile. She is a chartered member of the Chartered Institute of Personnel Directors. Until recently, she was Head of Leadership Development at the Institute of Education. She is now an independent consultant and works with many international schools across the world, as both a trainer and a consultant.

Jenny Francis

Dr Jenny Francis has worked in schools for over 30 years in a variety of roles, from class teacher to head teacher and in supporting schools for the local authority. She now works as a leadership trainer and coach, supporting and challenging schools to raise achievement for all, mainly in London.

Sue Hellman

Sue is Director of UK Consultancy and Knowledge Transfer at the London Centre for Leadership in Learning (LCLL), Institute of Education. She has extensive knowledge and experience of leading and managing change within schools and other educational organisations. Sue was a head teacher of a junior school with a specialised unit for children with emotional and behavioural difficulties and has undertaken two acting headships in schools in challenging circumstances. As a Regional Programme Leader for London for the Training and Development Agency, Sue supported local authorities and schools to implement the change agenda. She is a coach for trainee head teachers on the National Professional Qualification for Headteachers (NPQH) programme, as well as a facilitator for a range of leadership programmes at LCLL. She is also a Primary School Improvement Advisor and Vice Chair of Governors at an Early Years Centre in Hertfordshire.

Kim Insley

Kim Insley is a lecturer, researcher, teacher, mother (to three boys) and a wife. These aspects reflect just a few dimensions of her identify and suggest the diversity of her work. Having worked with children from ages 3 to 11, she stepped into Higher Education. Currently, she is Director of the IoE Short Courses unit and Programme Director of the Advanced Educational Practice programme. She now travels further afield to run professional development courses as well as courses in schools across the UK. Her research explores the development of professionalism and relationships between teachers and other adults working with children and supporting children's access to the curriculum.

Louise Ishani

Louise Ishani has a background in primary school leadership in Inner London. In 2002, Louise moved into education and leadership consultancy work, setting up her own company called Integrity First Training. Louise is co-author of published research into good practice in raising the achievement of black pupils. Louise worked as a consultant for the DfE and Primary National Strategy, advising both LAs and schools and developing materials focused on raising the achievement of black pupils. Louise has also worked nationally on leadership development programmes for teachers and head teachers.

Pauline Lyons

Pauline Lyons has worked in education for nearly 35 years. During this time, she has taught in primary, secondary and special schools and was a head teacher of a Church of England primary school in south London. For the past five years, she has worked as a consultant in London boroughs developing local authorities' strategies for support staff and has trained teaching assistants and parent support advisers. Pauline has also facilitated the National College for School Leadership's course 'Leading from the Middle' for the London Centre for Leadership in Learning.

Douglas McIldowie

Douglas was head teacher of a comprehensive school for 14 years, and early in his headship he was invited to pilot what was then known as Local Financial Management (LFM). His experience of pioneering strategic financial planning and management has informed his chapter in this book. Since retiring from headship, he has tutored, trained and coached several hundred aspiring head teachers on the NPQH programme.

Graham and Barbara Saltmarsh

Graham Saltmarsh is a freelance inspector working on behalf of Ofsted. A former senior Scotland Yard detective officer, he completed his police career as a member of the inspectorate for the National Crime Squads of England and Wales. He has particular expertise in leadership and management, community cohesion and safeguarding. He is a governor of a large secondary school. Barbara Saltmarsh is also a freelance inspector working on behalf of Ofsted. A former head teacher of an Inner London primary school, she is a consultant and tutor, facilitator, coach and mentor for the National College for School Leadership. Her particular areas of expertise are in leadership and management, curriculum, school improvement, and teaching and learning. She is a magistrate for the East Kent Bench.

Carol Taylor

Carol Taylor is Programme Leader: Strategic Professional Development at the London Centre for Leadership in Learning at the Institute of Education. She is currently working with PD leaders across London and nationally, and has been involved as a consultant on the national TDA project, looking at effective professional development practices. Carol's background is in school leadership teams.

Linda Trapnell

Linda has 40 years' experience in education. For 10 years, she was a head teacher and is now an independent consultant at GLT Associates. She has spoken at education and business conferences in London, Dubai, Mexico, Belfast and Kuala Lumpur. Linda is an expert in conflict resolution in education and business settings, training teachers and company employees. She also promotes leadership and management skills across the UK and Europe and in the Middle East.

Part I

Leading and Managing the School Workforce

Leading and Managing People

Mary Dawe

Talk to any head teacher, line manager or head of department and they will tell you that their biggest challenge is to do with the people they lead or manage: they are resisting change; they are not skilled enough; they are lacking motivation.

There is a saying in Yorkshire: 'Everyone's queer but thee and me, and thou's a bit strange'. The problem is that we are complex creatures with different needs, motivators and background and behaviours. Learning to understand other people is the key to successful leadership.

In this chapter, we will consider the following:

- Trust
- Know thyself
- Building a positive culture
- Developing a clear vision
- Building on strengths
- Developing others
- Holding to account
- Leadership styles and when to use them
- Developing coaching and mentoring

Trust

I think the main issue is trust. Working as I do with many groups of middle leaders and trainee head teachers, I see that there is often a lack of trust between senior and middle leadership or within a subject area or a year group. To develop trust, one needs to be trustworthy – worthy of trust – and this takes time. It is achieved in the following ways:

- **Respect others** – no matter what their status
- **Involve others and seek their input** – if you want buy-in
- **Help people to learn skills** – continuous professional development
- **Do the right thing** – working with integrity
- **Be consistent** – not treating everyone the same but treating everyone fairly
- **Share information** – too many leaders keep secrets as a power tool
- **Tell the truth** – again acting with integrity
- **Admit mistakes** – one of the best ways to avoid a blame culture
- **Give and receive constructive feedback** – the emphasis is on constructive
- **Maintain confidentiality** – when appropriate

A friend of mine took over as head teacher in an inner-city primary school where there had been a strong blame culture. She said that in order to break that culture she had to show it was OK to take risks and to get things wrong occasionally. She had to say things like, 'I won't do that assembly again; it didn't go very well at all'. People gradually learnt that it was all right to make mistakes – but it took a long time to build that trust.

If trust is in place, then holding others to account becomes less difficult because people will know that you are fair, that you have integrity.

In his 2006 book, *The Speed of Trust*, Stephen Covey explains that lack of trust costs the US economy millions of dollars per year, because where there is no trust all work procedures take much longer. Hargreaves (1994: 424) states that active trust means that teachers 'feel a stronger obligation towards and responsibility for their colleagues'. In other words, trust creates interdependence.

Know thyself

Understanding others is complex and the first step in that direction is to know yourself. Ask yourself some of these questions:

- Do you understand and have control over your own emotions?
- Do you understand the emotions of others? Do you have empathy? (These questions are about emotional intelligence.)
- Are you values driven? What are your values? What do you care about?
- Do you understand your own moral purpose?
- Can you articulate these values?

Being able to understand where you are coming from is linked to your integrity; if people understand that your decisions are not just arbitrary but are value-driven, then they will respect you. Some leaders worry about articulating their values, fearing conflict but, as Bennis and Thomas argue,

When an organisation's values are clear, participant's perceptions tend to be more accurate and decision making tends to be simpler and faster. Organisations with clear shared values outperform their peers. And values are less likely to be divisive if everyone remembers that tolerance is a key value in a diverse workplace. (2007)

Having clear values gives clarity to your teachers. As Peters and Waterman comment: 'People way down the line know what they are supposed to do in most situations because the handful of guiding principles are crystal clear' (1995: 76).

Geoff Southworth (2008) reminds us of the importance of re-examining our values:

Leadership is a social activity and professional leadership should be based on sound professional knowledge and judgements, not shallow opinions, or with scant regard to evidence, or experience. The underpinning values should be surfaced, interrogated and challenged from time to time, otherwise they become habitual and remain untested.

Building a positive culture

At its simplest, culture is 'the way we do things round here' (Deal and Kennedy, 1982). This refers to the set of unspoken rules and values that form over time and guide organisational behaviour. Imagine the reception area of your school. What values are apparent? Who is allowed to go into this area? What does this tell you?

The climate of the school is 'how it feels to work round here' (Deal and Kennedy, 1982) – it is about people's feelings, expectations and impressions of what it is like to work in a particular place.

As a leader, you can have a great influence on the culture and climate of your school, faculty or department. You can make decisions about the environment but, more importantly, you can choose how you deal with people. You can choose to be respectful, always calm. You can choose to greet people when you meet them; you can choose to notice the good things you see instead of looking for the bad. When things go wrong, instead of searching for blame, you can say, 'How can we make it right? How can we make sure it doesn't happen again?'

I visit many schools in my job and there are plenty that I look forward to visiting because of the warmth of welcome and the positive energy which they exude. Children greet teachers; teachers greet children and each other. The message being given is: people matter. As you walk round the school, you can almost hear the buzz coming from classrooms. Young people's work is all over the walls.

In contrast, there are schools where I can't get past a very unwelcoming receptionist; where no one makes eye contact; where, when I walk round the school, there are children in corridors getting out of lessons; there is little display and what there is, is torn. Which of these schools would you want your child or a friend's child to attend?

Culture and climate can affect the motivation of both teachers and pupils and can impact on achievement. Deal and Kennedy (1982) and Deal and Peterson (1998) illustrated how dysfunctional school cultures, e.g. inward focus, short-term focus, low morale, fragmentation, inconsistency, emotional outbursts, and subculture values that supersede shared organisational values, can impede organisational improvement.

Take a renewed look at the culture and climate of your school, faculty, key stage, year group or department and ask yourself these questions:

1   Look at one room – what do you hear or see that tells you about the underpinning values?
2   Look at your school brochure and/or your website. What are the main messages? Are they a reality? What do you need to do to make them a reality?
3   Think of the last time something went wrong. How did you handle it? Is there a blame culture?
4   How do you know if someone has a good idea? Would you listen to them?
5   How are teachers treated? Are they respected?

Developing a clear vision

If you are a leader, you need to lead people somewhere. Do you know where you are going? What do you want your school to look like in a year's time? In three years' time? That's your vision – your image of a desired future. As I visit schools, I often ask, 'What's your school's vision?' Few teachers and even fewer students can articulate it ... To develop an inspiring vision that gives a clear sense of mission is very important for the development of a school.

The best way to develop a vision that is owned by all is to create a process that involves everyone. A visualisation exercise is a good way to start. What would you see, hear, be saying if your school had outstanding teaching and learning? What would teachers be seeing, hearing, saying and doing? What would students be seeing, hearing, saying and doing?

To have an agreed vision is not easy – it will require all your leadership skills – but to have a shared sense of purpose is crucial to real school improvement. Mark Leppard, Principal of Doha College, A British International School in Qatar, has been working on vision. He began by asking his board of governors to think about what the school stands for and what it could be. He asked the same questions of parents through an annual open forum and all teachers and students via assemblies. The data was collated and used as the basis for a meeting with the senior leadership team (SLT) and the board of governors. At the end of that meeting, they had a rough draft of Vision, Mission and Core Values. At a whole staff meeting, the principal and the Chair of Governors presented the drafts. Teachers then broke into team groups to draw up their own Vision, Mission and Core Values. All this data was collated again and, at another meeting of the SLT and board of governors, a final version was agreed. This was again shown to staff to check there were no strong objections and that everyone felt they could work in this direction. Finally, the finished drafts were sent to parents and students.

Of course, vision on its own is simply a daydream without action. Mission is the way the school will implement the vision; I like to think of the vision as the destination on a journey. I need an action plan (development plan) to help me get to my destination. I need to take people on my journey with me but, as long as everyone is clear about the destination, some people may come a different route.

You need to keep communicating your vision so that everyone is clear about it. All this time you will have been using what Daniel Goleman (Goleman et al., 2002) calls a visionary leadership style – mobilising others towards a vision. Once you have your vision, the style becomes even more important in keeping the vision alive and in people's minds. One head teacher I know asks of every new suggestion, 'And how does that fit into our vision?' She constantly reminds people of their vision. Doha College has made this a question in performance management, where they ask, 'In your job last year, how did you support the Vision, Mission and Core Values of the college?' In recruitment, they ask candidates how they could contribute to the Vision, Mission and Core Values – it ensures a buy-in from new staff. Similar questions are asked at the Head Boy/Girl interviews. They have monitoring days where students and parents are asked how they intend to support the Vision, Mission and Core Values of the college. I think keeping the vision as a living, working thing with students is also important. When I last visited Doha College, Year 10 students were creating posters to describe the vision.

You need to empower others to take action on your vision. This is where you put your vision into action. As a leader, you will begin to see changes being planned or made. You need to check that teachers and support staff have the necessary skills to deal with these changes. If not, do you need to plan a training programme? Similarly, do you have the necessary resources to implement the change? At one junior school I know, the entire staff were told that next term they would all need to teach French. The worry and fear this caused was immense because no one had checked the skills of the staff. Another school held a Professional Development Day and countless meetings to introduce a new reading scheme, only to find that the books took another half term to arrive. This caused a great deal of frustration.

Middle managers will need to create their own vision based on the whole-school vision and they will need to contextualise and give details to the development plan. What does this mean for my department/year group/faculty/key stage? What will it look like in my context? What can my team do to realise the vision? Are there other aspects which are subject-specific that need to be part of your team's vision but not of the whole-school vision? Harris concludes that a one-size-fits-all model will not work because: 'The context in which people work and learn together is where they construct and refine meaning leading to a shared purpose or set of goals' (2002: 24).

You will also need to monitor how the mission is being carried out and frequently review both your progress so far and your vision. Have circumstances changed so that we need to adjust our vision?

Building on strengths

To realise your vision, you need to work with the team you have. In his 2001 book, *From Good to Great*, Jim Collins talks about 'getting the right people on the bus'. This is great advice for recruitment – and you are very lucky if you are starting in a new school – but most of us have to work with people already on the bus. The most important thing is to get to know the other staff, so find out what makes them tick, what they care about in education and what their strengths are. You might already have a view about what they are good at but ask. Some people hide their lights and others don't think skills they demonstrated in previous careers are likely to be relevant. Work to their strengths – this is particularly important with blockers, those who are against change. Use their strengths positively. People are often afraid of change, yet they have years of relevant experience they can use if they are encouraged.

Once you have identified people's strengths, you can extend and build on them through professional development.

Developing others

A good school is a school that learns. To ensure school improvement and retention of staff, you have to commit to professional development. You need to decide what professional development is needed in order to create your vision. Professional development is not just about sending people on courses or organising whole-school development. You could consider any of the following:

- giving people time to research topics
- peer observations or expert observations

- visits to other schools
- shadowing
- coaching/mentoring
- action research.

Dylan William talks about how difficult it is to make changes in classroom practice when behaviours are entrenched and have become the default way of working:

> *For example, a few months ago, an elementary school teacher in northern New Jersey was telling me about her efforts to change her questioning techniques. She wanted to use popsicle sticks with students' names on them as a way of choosing students to answer her questions at random—a technique that increases student engagement and elicits answers from a broad range of students instead of just the usual suspects. However, she was having difficulty calling on specific students because she automatically started most questions with phrases like, 'Does anyone know ...?' Frustrated, she wondered why she was finding this simple change so difficult. This teacher has been teaching for 25 years, and we worked out that, over her career, she has probably asked around half a million questions. When you've done something one way half a million times, doing it another way is going to be pretty difficult! (2008: 38).*

William recommends teachers working in Teacher Learning Communities to try out new ways of working in groups. He suggests these groups should:

be planned for two years

start with volunteers

meet monthly for at least 75 minutes

aim for a group size of 8–10

group with similar assignments

ask teachers to make modest, brief action plans. (William, 2008)

Whether you are the head of a school or a senior or middle leader, you cannot do everything yourself. You must develop leadership skills in others. Too often, when teachers are promoted into early leadership positions, they are promoted because of their subject knowledge or their ability in the classroom and are not given guidance in leading and managing people. Alma Harris et al. (2001) found this to be the case. Here are ways in which two schools planned to develop their leaders.

We start with a list provided by the head teacher of Willow Girls School, a school in North London:

- new staff induction – people who are promoted internally are also inducted into their new role
- annual middle leader conferences
- leadership visits – middle leaders visit other London schools
- outreach work through ASTs
- Leadership Team Secondments – middle leaders apply for a year's secondment on the senior leadership team (SLT)
- Leading from the Middle, Leadership Pathways, Tomorrow's Leaders, and other National College courses.

At Holly School in East London, middle leaders who have completed the National College programme, Leading from the Middle, go on to shadow the role of senior leaders and begin to share the role as the senior leader nears retirement. The school feels it is growing its own leaders.

However, head teachers need to be aware that if they are investing in developing their leaders they are likely to get developed leaders – leaders who end up knocking on any artificial ceilings there are in the school. They may be more comfortable with collaborative learning, with leading a project, with coaching, with creating new ideas and may wish to develop these attributes further. It is increasingly important that schools respond to this. Here is HMIE in Scotland talking about distributive leadership:

> The most effective way to perform the range of functions required within complex establishments is by sharing responsibility for leadership. The Integrated Children's Service policy and practice agenda has increased the demand for shared leadership development as a way of supporting joint working. The scale and pace of change is increasing the demand for leaders at various levels and a broadening of the scale of practice. We are seeing a growing shift towards equally responsive and flexible leadership patterns. The practice of leadership has become something that is within the power of every member of staff and not something that only senior staff do. (HMIE, 2007)

In a school where leadership is developed, staff are helped to make an impact on a wider school; ideas from every level are taken up and championed; it is easy to share ideas and people are aware of what is happening elsewhere.

Holding to account

So far we have discussed: trusting staff; dealing with staff in a positive manner and creating a positive culture and climate; creating a shared vision; building on strengths; and developing others. However, there will be times when you will need to hold people to account. I do not intend to deal with this in detail as my colleague Linda Trapnell will give this full attention in her chapter in this book (Chapter 3). However, it is worth reiterating that if you are explicit about your values, if you set a clear vision, if you set clear standards, then people know what is expected of them. You must therefore deal with teachers who are not doing their job. I have been talking about your leadership responsibility to teachers but your first responsibility is to the students in your school, and if their education is suffering then you must deal with it.

Leadership styles and when to use them

Daniel Goleman (Goleman et al., 2002) lists six leadership styles to describe the way in which you interact with those you lead. You are likely to have a default style but no style is right or wrong. You need to use the right style in the right context with the right person.

Commanding

You are basically saying 'Do it'. Use sparingly. This style will not get people on board but you may need to use it if you have a crisis or if you have to make a stand on a non-negotiable issue. For example, Ofsted are coming in three days' time and you want to make sure everyone has read the final version of a new policy you have all agreed. You don't go into discussion, you just say, 'Would everyone please ensure they have read and are familiar with our learning and teaching policy'. Another example of using commanding is when you have had resistance to something you consider to be important. If after a lot of talking there is still resistance, then you have to say, 'Just do it!'

Visionary

Here you are saying 'Come with me'. For any leader, a visionary style is crucial. You are creating learning opportunities so that young people are ready for a world we do not know. Your vision has the potential to inspire and enthuse staff to move forward. The only time I would advise caution in using this style is when you have staff in your team who hate change, who defend the past with fervour. These people do not need big pictures; they need small steps described so you can link the future to the past.

Pace-setting

You may well use this style when you are implementing change. You model what you want to see and expect others to do as you do. It can be very positive if used for a relatively short time. However, it prevents flexibility and creativity, so be careful how long you use this style for. If you have people who are strong advocates of your plans for change, this style could have a negative impact.

Affiliative

This style is giving the message that people matter. You get to know your team and you show you care about their welfare. 'How is your son, is he better?', 'Did you have a good weekend?', 'I don't want you working late on your birthday.' All of these are examples of using an affiliative style. Many people respond positively to this style but beware of being too affiliative. If you overuse this style, you could have trouble holding people to account.

Democratic

You are using a democratic style when you are asking for and taking note of the opinions of all in your team. You will not be able to use this style all the time as it can be quite time-consuming but people generally respond well to it. It is likely to induce buy-in to the change as people will think that they matter.

Coaching

The coaching style is one that develops others and shows respect and belief in the ideas of others. I recently saw it used to great effect in a school where a teacher came into the head's office about a problem with a pupil. The head said, 'What do you think you should do?' The teacher replied with a suggestion. The head said, 'Is there any reason why you shouldn't do that?' She was silent for a few moments and then said, 'I'll go and do it,' and off she went. This style is not as time-consuming as you might suppose and can induce huge buy-in and commitment because you have shown respect and belief in your team. There will be a few people who will not respond to this. They will be the ones who want you to give them all the answers. If you persevere with coaching for them, you may affect a change but it will take time. Coaching can empower others to feel they can achieve.

Developing coaching and mentoring

Using a coaching leadership style is very effective but coaching in its fuller context is also an effective way of developing yourself and others. If you are really interested in this aspect, I suggest you read one of the many specialist books on coaching but I will give you an outline of some of the general principles here.

Coaching is strongly promoted by the TDA and National College. Within the current TDA teaching standards, people are expected to be coached throughout their working careers from trainee teacher, through to NQT and head teacher. These standards also indicate that we need to have coaching skills and to apply these in our working context.

The National College has coaching in all its leadership programmes. The application of coaching and mentoring is now encouraged as a way of supporting learning and development, whether this is related to classroom practice, broader aspects of professional/career development or as a way of developing and distributing leadership within school.

There are a plethora of definitions of coaching and mentoring with little consistency between them. Some definitions of coaching are similar in nature to other definitions of mentoring. However, mentoring is often seen as incorporating a focus on knowledge sharing and directing less experienced staff. It is about longer-term development and life transitions. Mentoring relationships are usually longer term. Coaching, meanwhile, is seen as being less dependent on the coach being an expert and more on the ability to facilitate the coachee's ability to gain insight, to learn, to change. Some would argue that coaching is more short-term focused; it is about enhancing performance or skills development.

Here are some definitions:

- 'Coaching is the art of facilitating the performance, learning and development of another.' (Downey, 1999)
- 'Coaching is unlocking a person's potential to maximize their own performance. It is helping them to learn rather than teaching them.' (Gallwey, 2000)
- 'Coaching focuses on future possibilities, not past mistakes.' (Whitmore, 2002)
- 'A collaborative, solution focussed, results orientated and systematic process in which the coach facilitates the enhancements of work performance, life experience, self directed learning and personal growth of the coachee.' (Grant, 2003)

The National Framework for Coaching and Mentoring, designed by Curee (www.curee-paccts.com/), gives the following definitions of specialist coaching and collaborative coaching (this second definition is not too far from Dylan William's notion of Teacher Learning Communities):

Specialist coaching is a structured, sustained process for enabling the development of a specific aspect of a professional learner's practice. Collaborative (Co-) coaching is a structured, sustained process between two or more professional learners to enable them to embed knowledge and skills from specialist sources in day to day practice. (Curee, 2005)

The concept of mentoring comes from Homer's *Odyssey*; Mentor was the older wise guide whom Odysseus left to help his son Telemachus. From this, we have taken the notion of an older, experienced person advising a younger, less experienced person. The National Framework describes it thus: 'Mentoring is a structured, sustained process for supporting professional learners through significant career transitions' (www.curee-paccts.com/).

Coaching presumes an equality of relationship; both coaching and mentoring are based on respect for the other person and a belief in the resourcefulness and potential of the other person. If we, with simplicity, and certainly going against a number of experts, think of mentoring as giving advice, then I intend in this next section to concentrate on coaching.

Jenny Rogers (2004) gives the following principles of coaching:

1   The client is resourceful.
2   The coach's role is to spring loose this resourcefulness.
3   Coaching addresses the whole person – past, present and future.
4   The client sets the agenda.
5   The coach and the client are equals.
6   Coaching is about change and action.

The last point I think is important. Coaching is not just about having a conversation. It is about having a structured conversation that leads to an outcome. This is why it is such a helpful tool in staff development. I personally think every leader at whatever level should have a coach, to help them reflect on what has happened and to develop their leadership capacity.

So how do you start this structured conversation? Well, first of all set out your parameters, your protocols. Coaching textbooks call this contracting. What are the rules of engagement? What subjects can we or can't we discuss? What is confidential, what isn't? What do we mean by confidential? How long have we got?

You can build rapport by:

- reflecting the learners' language (visual, auditory, kinesthetic)
- body language – attentiveness and mirroring (non-mimicking)
- pacing – matching pace of conversation
- creating a safe environment/trust
- empathy
- time (list compiled by Julia Foster Turner).

In coaching, we must really listen, putting aside our inner voice, but really listening for meaning. Don't rely on directed listening, where the listener is concentrating to make sense of what the speaker is saying – relating what they hear to their own experiences to give sympathy or so that they can next argue their point of view but try to listen for the learner – where you suspend your own judgement and inner dialogue so that you are entirely present to the learner/client. There are huge benefits to just listening to people, but to help people move forward you often need to ask them questions. There are different types of questions:

- Clarifying – 'Tell me more about …'
- Reflective questions – getting people to think: 'What would have to change in order for …?'

- Summarising questions – checking for understanding: 'So, you are saying that ...?'
- Outcome questions – 'What could be your first step in taking this forward?'

Some basic rules of thumb when thinking about questioning:

- Avoid closed questions – use open questions wherever possible.
- Set short questions – not two or three questions in one.
- Don't make it advice in disguise! ('Haven't you ...?' 'Would it ...?')
- Avoid leading questions, such as those that would take them to the 'answer' you think would help them, e.g. 'Would you agree that from what you have said so far ...?' (Rules developed by Julia Foster Turner)

Remember that it is your client's agenda, not yours; you are raising your client's awareness and promoting their thinking. Don't be afraid of challenging their thinking – and encourage them to take responsibility for themselves.

Conclusion

I started this chapter by saying that many leaders view working with people as the biggest challenge. It is the biggest joy as a leader when you see people develop their own leadership and see that you and your team are really making a difference to the children in your school. It is worth persevering. You need patience, resilience and, most of all, time. Good luck!

Questions for further thinking

- What do you see as your strengths in leading and managing people?
- What areas would you like to develop, and how are you going to do this?
- Is there a person on your team with whom you are having difficulty? Are there strategies that you might try to help you deal with this person better?

Resources and useful further reading

- Goleman, D., Boyatzis, R. and Kee, A. (2002) *The New Leaders*. London: Time Warner – a clear explanation of the importance of emotional intelligence and the use of leadership styles.
- Kouznes, J. and Posner, B. (2003) *Encouraging the Heart*. San Francisco: Jossey-Bass – a good guide to developing people.

- Starr, J. (2011) *The Coaching Manual*, 3rd edition. Harlow: Prentice Hall – a good practical reference book on coaching.
- www.thenationalcollege.org – join their leadership library for a wealth of material on leadership.

References

Bennis, W. and Thomas, R.J. (2007) *Leading for a Lifetime*. Boston, MA: Harvard Business School.

Collins, J. (2001) *From Good to Great*. London: Random House.

Covey, S.M.R. (2006) *The Speed of Trust*. London: Simon and Schuster.

Curee (2005) *National Framework for Mentoring and Coaching*. Available at: http://www.curee.co.uk/resources/publications/national-framework-mentoring-and-coaching

Deal, T. and Kennedy, A. (1982) *Corporate Cultures*. San Francisco: Perseus Publishing.

Deal, T. and Peterson, K. (1998) How Leaders Influence the Culture of Schools, *Educational Leadership* 56(1): 28–30.

Downey, M. (1999) *Effective Coaching*. London: Orion Business Toolkit.

Gallwey, T. (2000) *The Inner Game of Work*. New York: Random House.

Goleman, D. et al. (2002) *The New Leaders*. London: Time Warner.

Grant, A.M. (2003) The Impact of Life Coaching on Goal Attainment, Metacognition and Mental Health, *Social Behavior and Personality* 31(3): 253–63.

Hargreaves, A. (1994) *Changing Teachers, Changing Times: Teachers' Work and Culture in the Post-modern Age*. London: Cassell.

Harris, A. (2002) Effective Leadership in Schools Facing Challenging Circumstances, *School Leadership and Management* 22(1): 15–27.

Harris, A. et al. (2001) Effective Training for Subject Leaders, *In Service Journal of Education* 1(27): 1.

HMIE (2007) *Leadership for Learning: The challenges of leading in a time of change*, Livingston, HMIE.

Homer, *The Odyssey*.

Peters, T. and Waterman, R.H. (1995) *In Search of Excellence*. London: HarperCollins.

Rogers, J. (2004) *Coaching Skills*. Milton Keynes: Open University Press.

Southworth, G. (2008) Primary Leadership Today and Tomorrow, *School Leadership and Management* 8(5).

Whitmore, J. (2002) *Coaching for Performance*, 3rd edition. London: Nicholas Brearley.

William, D. (2008) Changing Classroom Practice, *Educational Leadership: Informative Assessment* 65(4): 36–62.

Wellbeing in Educational Settings

Domini Bingham

In this chapter, we will consider the following:

- Why wellbeing matters
- Planning for wellbeing
- Putting wellbeing into action
- Sustaining wellbeing

This chapter focuses on wellbeing for the organisation, rather than on the individual, in supporting good practice necessary to improve wellbeing in the workplace. Research has shown that attending to the wellbeing of staff can ultimately improve effectiveness for students, while positive feelings of wellbeing also affect retention of staff to provide a sustainable workforce.

Ideas around wellbeing are not new. Many of today's ideas around wellbeing, such as happiness in the positive psychology movement made popular through the work of Martin Seligman, take their starting point from Aristotle and the concept of wellbeing been seen as holistic, as about wider notions of what it means for humans to flourish.

Why wellbeing matters

Staff in educational settings are under ever more pressure in the workplace, and so leading for wellbeing in educational organisations is an important area of study. Research conducted in schools in the UK (PricewaterhouseCoopers (PWC), 2007) shows that 44 per cent of teachers found their job very or extremely stressful and 90 per cent of respondents advised of an increase in stress levels. Stress and work-related illness affect teacher retention, exacerbated where teachers feel they are unappreciated or uninvolved in decision making. Issues that are often raised include increased workload, structural reorganisation and countless initiatives. There is a growing research available on wellbeing for the general workplace and for wellbeing in education organisations (Gold, 2004; NCSL, 2009; PWC, 2007).

Wellbeing is subjective and there is no one clear definition. Indeed, there is no consensus about whether it is one word or two! For some, it is quality of life; for others, it is about work–life balance, and for yet others, stress. However, what is stressful to one person may not be to another (Teacher Support Network (TSN)). In the wider context and in the classroom, wellbeing can be divided into: physical, emotional, mental, intellectual and spiritual.

The role of stress

There are also many definitions of stress but a key one is a feeling of not coping. However, we know that some stress is good for wellbeing and helps motivate and energise. A distinction can be made between good stress and bad stress (called distress). The Health and Safety Executive (HSE) define (bad) stress as 'the adverse reaction people have to excessive pressures or other types of demand placed on them'(2003). What is clear is that the perception of a situation as stressful is complex as it is individual and dependent on each person's context and on their specific personality characteristics. Therefore, great care needs to be taken in not dismissing individual emotional needs and requirements.

The point made is that stress is not, in fact, a medical condition and a certain level of stress is desirable in some situations. It helps motivate people, boosting productivity. However, when the pressure exceeds a person's ability to cope, it turns into a negative experience rather than a positive one. Stress, particularly prolonged exposure, results in symptoms of anxiety, depression, sleeplessness and inability to switch off or relax among others.

However, what also needs to be remembered is that some stress may be non-work related – possibly due to pressures in home life – but employers cannot afford to say that is outside their remit. Occupational health has to consider and offer some solutions for staff's outside stress too, as the situation outside of work can rapidly affect what is going on inside work through falling performance, absences and changes in behaviour.

National and international perspectives and policy

There is a recognised link between how an organisation is managed and the wellbeing of staff. An organisation that places staff wellbeing at its core will have reduced staff turnover, increased staff retention and a more motivated and fulfilled workforce (TSN).

Wellbeing for staff is also important in the knock-on effect it has on students. It contributes to a virtuous circle, linked to effectiveness of teachers, which in turn has been shown to contribute to positive effects on student outcomes. International research across eight education systems into developing future leadership capacity, shows clear evidence that developing teachers makes the biggest contribution to student learning outcomes (Barber et al., 2010).

Also important is the key role leaders play in wellbeing. In education settings, research links wellbeing of the school workforce and the role of the school leader in helping to improve student performance. Within schools, the international literature shows that one of the most important ways in which school leaders contribute to teaching and learning is 'through their impact on the motivation, development and wellbeing of staff' (PWC, 2007).

In England, policies around wellbeing are either implicit or present in a number of strategic planning documents for education settings – first, through the self-evaluation tool in schools, structured around Ofsted's eight themes for self-evaluation. Self-evaluation is a well-established activity in maintained schools in England and forms the basis for planning for development and improvement. Inspection takes account of and contributes to a school's self-evaluation. The Every Child Matters agenda is a shared programme of change to improve outcomes for all children and young people whose five ECM outcomes relate to and cover a number of Articles of the UN Convention on the Rights of the Child (UNCRC) which are:

- Be healthy.
- Make a positive contribution.
- Stay safe.
- Achieve economic wellbeing.
- Enjoy and achieve.

The Ofsted framework for inspection takes into account seven pupil outcomes – the five Every Child Matters outcomes above and *two* more:

- Pupils' behaviour
- Spiritual development
- Moral development } considered as *one* outcome
- Social development
- Cultural development

Wellbeing is also present in the UK government's framework for sustainable schools, with many schools looking at the type of food they offer, encouraging healthy ways to come to school, and making schools more energy-efficient. Since April 2011 in England, the well-established healthy schools programme has been school-led and many schools have already achieved the national healthy school status. A Healthy Schools whole-school review has *nine* headings by which your school can be measured for provision and school improvement for children and young people's health and wellbeing. Of the nine headings, *one* relates specifically to staff continuing professional development (CPD) needs, health and wellbeing (DfE, 2011). This review can therefore be considered as part of a self-evaluation plan.

As the pace of working life has quickened so has the increase in stress, particularly work-related stress. The importance of a society's wellbeing is now being measured alongside GDP measurement at European level, in particular the importance of subjective wellbeing – how people actually feel they are progressing in life, how anxious or depressed they are feeling and how satisfied they feel they are with their lives.

The OECD has set guidelines on the collection of wellbeing statistics, asking questions about:

- life satisfaction
- positive and negative effects
- purpose, meaning and flourishing.

In summary, measuring wellbeing in organisations and introducing policies to tackle and reduce stress can make a real difference to employee wellbeing. International organisations are now taking note of the importance of wellbeing. There is also a legal requirement in some countries under health and safety laws to conduct a risk assessment for work-related stress and establish measures to counteract and reduce the risks identified.

Questions for reflection

- What CPD opportunities, relevant to health and wellbeing, do your staff have access to this year?
- How does your organisation identify staff CPD needs of relevance to health and wellbeing?
- What will you be doing or what have you done about the needs identified?

Teachers and self-efficacy

The key to what makes good teachers is the notion of self-efficacy (Bangs, 2011), which can be seen as a response to the straight-jacketing of the conditions of target setting, which Bangs says can reduce a teacher's self-efficacy. An element of wellbeing, self-efficacy is the extent to which 'beliefs determine how people feel, think, motivate themselves and behave' and is also related to 'beliefs about their capabilities to produce designated levels of performance that exercise influence over events that affect their lives'. Self-efficacy has been shown to affect work in a number of environments, including the education sector and teacher's actions in the classroom. Self-efficacy can be seen within the overall category of wellbeing, as it is linked to wider ideas of flourishing and wellbeing.

Wiliam (2010) suggests that if you care about raising student achievement, then it is important to improve teacher quality and that means you have to improve the quality of existing teachers.

Questions for reflection

- What does William's suggestion (above) say to you?
- What issues does this raise for you?
- What do you draw upon for guidance around wellbeing?

Planning for wellbeing

- Wellbeing in the workplace – leading strategically
- What is the vision for your school?
- How are you communicating wellbeing?

In an independent study into school leadership (PWC, 2007), one of the key findings around developing and managing people was:

> that many school leaders have embraced these challenges in relation to people development well, but also that there is more to be done, at both institution and system level. For example, when head teachers were asked what their priorities should be going forward, as well as what their future skills needs were, staff management, recruitment and retention appeared quite far down the list.

> Whilst this is understandable given their other commitments, it nevertheless suggests that many school leaders may not have embraced the people agenda as fully as has been the case in other sectors (e.g. in the private sector where it is one of the bedrocks on which all current thinking on leadership is based). (PWC, 2007, page 5)

Questions for reflection

- What is your role as leader here?
- What do effective leaders do?
- As a leader, how does your own wellbeing impact on your colleagues?

Gold's (2004) research shows good school leaders manage to articulate, promote and encourage values in their leadership by: working with, managing and searching out change; keeping staff informed; working very closely with leadership groups; and developing leadership capacity and responsibility throughout their schools. Although more challenging to realise this in times of budgetary cuts, Gold's (2004) research shows that there is scope to reduce work stress. The level of control that employees are given and the supportiveness of the work environment helps in reducing the negative pressures of work.

Leadership also requires an ability to manage emotionally as well as intellectually. Leaders of schools today need to encompass values-based leadership and emotions-based leadership. Crawford (2009) says that 'Educational leadership is fundamentally about people, and people necessarily work in an emotional context, intrapersonally and interpersonally' (page 24).

Questions for reflection

- What is the vision for your setting? Why is it important? What are the challenges? How do you want to be in 12 months' time?
- What are your objectives?
- How are you communicating your objectives?
- How does your style of leadership impact on the wellbeing of others?

A focus on wellbeing

Research was conducted on the success shown, in very challenging circumstances, in a primary school which placed staff wellbeing at the centre of school improvement. The research showed that what works best is when 'heads provided a rich variety of professional learning and development opportunities for staff as part of their twin drive to raise standards and sustain motivation and commitment' (National College/TDA, 2010).

Putting wellbeing into action

Elements of good practice

1. What do you need to think about?

In work developed with educational leaders at the LCLL, these wellbeing and work–life balance organisational issues were most cited as areas for development:

- talent management
- stress management
- developing a coaching culture for empowerment
- change management and organisational development
- sustainable environments
- communicating with your staff using emotional leadership
- developing professional communities.

A four-year study in 2008 from the Chartered Institute of Personnel and Development (CIPD), into line management behaviour and stress at work, came up with four main areas as being the most important for wellbeing in the workplace:

- **Respect and responsibility:** relationship awareness – treating staff with respect, managing emotions and being considerate; the setting of realistic deadlines; giving more positive than negative feedback; considering work–life balance.
- **Managing the workload:** communicating tasks and objectives clearly; monitoring workloads; dealing with problems; being decisive; keeping staff involved, especially during periods of uncertainty, pressure and difficult financial conditions.
- **Managing the individual in the team:** a willingness to share something of yourself with your team; being available; being able to show authenticity as a leader and being able to socialise and show your heart.
- **Managing in difficult situations:** showing collaborative support in the management of wellbeing; being able to deal with conflict, and being willing to seek outside help and advice to resolve situations.

What is clear is that leadership involves attending to the work–life balance of staff and empowering teams to be effective.

The HSE (2003) has developed a six-standard framework which supports a wellbeing programme. These are set out in the table on the next page allowing you to consider where your organisation is at in developing a programme.

Table 2.1 *Where is your organisation at?*

Management Standard	1	2	3	4	5
Demands: workload, work patterns and work environment, work–life balance					
Control over how much say a person has in the way work is done					
Relationships: promoting positive working to avoid conflict and dealing with unacceptable behaviour					
Roie(s): do people understand their roles? Does an organisation ensure that roles are not conflicting?					
Change: how change is positively managed and communicated in an organisation					
Support: the degree to which encouragement, sponsorship and resources are provided by line management, colleagues and the organisation					

Note: 1 = starting out, 5 = firmly established.

2. Explore where your organisation is on the scale

Sharing strategies through thinking and reflecting

With colleagues, identify where on the scale you are. If you are starting out, you will be at 1 or 2. Choose a point between 1 and 5, representing where you want to shift to, if you have already embedded a wellbeing action plan. As a result, what three steps do you need to take to move on?

1 What do you need to do?
2 Who do you need to talk to?
3 By when?

The importance of organisational culture

Creating an educational organisation that is based on values means developing a culture of sharing, collaborating, expectations and mechanisms for sharing decision making. Culture makes or breaks an organisation. A culture which empowers adds value, empowering and enabling others to take on changes knowing they are valued. However, a culture that operates a command and control model will not enable others when changes are imposed and will result in further stress and reduced effectiveness. It is essential to recognise where you are on the journey, to capture it and promote it at every opportunity.

Being able to lead in a climate of change has been the subject of much study. Fullan (National College, 2009) notes the complexities of leading in a relentless focus of change and of the need for 're-culturing' of a school to support long-lasting, sustainable change.

3. Try to develop practice that places people's wellbeing at the centre of an organisation – this helps to create a more positive working environment

- Work on developing, encouraging and sustaining a culture where open and honest communication is encouraged. You will see the results in a culture where support and mutual respect are part of everyday work life.
- An organisation should aim to develop a work culture where everyone is treated with respect and dignity and where there is a zero tolerance approach to bullying.

The importance of trust in organisations

Stephen Covey (2006) sees trust as a crucial component in an organisation's culture. Trust impacts on us at all times and underpins everything we do, affecting the quality of all our relationships, all our communication and on every activity. At its basic level, trust means having confidence, while mistrust means suspicion.

The dividends of having high trust are, according to Covey (2006:19):

When trust is high, the dividend you receive is like a performance multiplier, elevating and improving every dimension of your organisation and your life ...

In a company, high trust materially improves communication, collaboration, execution, innovation, strategy, engagement, partnering, and relationships with all stakeholders.

Conversely, there are quantifiable costs that can be attributed to low trust. The economist Francis Fukuyama (in Covey, 2006) suggests that a widespread distrust in society ... imposes a kind of tax on all forms of economic activity, a tax that high-trust societies do not have to pay.

For an organisation, low levels of trust impact by the 'discounting' – that is the discarding – of what people say, which acts as a form of invisible tax on the organisation as leaders do not take into account what staff members say.

How can trust be grown?

Trust needs to start with the leadership. Covey (2006) says the number one job of a leader is to inspire trust. This requires leaders to look at their leadership styles and how they are perceived. It requires being consistent in building trust between and across the organisation. By using an alignment of a framework of elements and behaviours seen as those belonging to a 'high' trust organisation, organisations can grow trust and confidence in people's integrity and actions, their capabilities and their track record.

Questions for reflection

- How would you rate the culture of trust in your setting? Good? Average? Poor?
- Does my organisation operate on tax dividends or tax deduction?
- Am I as an individual a tax dividend or a tax deduction in my life?

---

4. Ideas for practice

- What kind of culture of trust do you want for your organisation?
- What steps are needed to reach this level?
- What time line will you put in place to achieve this?

Educational culture and environment

Two further areas taken from the healthy schools plan which can be used in the school improvement plan are worth considering in terms of how the environment impacts on staff wellbeing.

5. Responding to the healthy schools initiative

- How does your school culture and environment enable engagement of the whole-school community, including staff?
- How does your school environment promote health and wellbeing in staff (for example, through access to clean and palatable drinking water and access to healthy food and drink in line with good practice)? (Adapted from *Healthy Schools Toolkit*, DfE, 2011)

Although the types of leadership research outlined above are for head teachers, we can see that the principle can be equally transferred to all parts of an organisation.

Table 2.2 *Identifying the gaps*

Involve the whole workforce in a series of group exercises to identify any gaps:
Where we are: --   **Where we want to be:** ---
Identify what wellbeing is for all staff and set some targets
Map and identify what is already taking place
Use the information to identify the gaps
Prioritise the gaps to be filled
Agree on the strategy and move forward to the action plan

(Adapted from NCSL/TDA *School Improvement Planning Framework, 2009/10*)

Developing an action plan

We can now consider tools useful in developing and prioritising solutions for enacting wellbeing. First, it is necessary to identify what is the state of health and wellbeing in your organisation. A health and wellbeing needs analysis will be useful in identifying any gaps and in determining priorities and developing outcomes. For this to work, all senior leaders need to be involved so the outcome is then adopted into the strategic planning of the organisation.

6. Preparing to engage

Elements of a wellbeing programme

The elements included will vary from context to context but some examples are:

- flexible work policies
- work–life balance
- assertiveness training
- balancing of roles and avoidance of role overload
- development of resilience; taking responsibility for own emotions/actions (using emotional intelligence (EQ))
- healthy relationships – managing conflict

Table 2.3 *Action planning for a one-year wellbeing programme*

Steps in implementing a wellbeing programme	Questions to reflect on (complete panel)
Clarify with senior leadership team to ensure that it is seen by all as of strategic importance	
Set staff orientation through internal communication	
Set up wellbeing team from across all faculties, to include a champion in each area	
Arrange staff meeting to launch wellbeing initiative and wellbeing survey	
Implement wellbeing survey for staff	
Consider the findings of the audit, focusing on four/five major elements	
Announce results to staff, asking for feedback and ensure you get buy-in	
In small network groups, led by champions, work to develop wellbeing action plan based on the results	
Prioritise as you won't be able to do everything all at once	
Put initial phase into action	
Survey the results after three months	
Evaluate and make changes where required	
Put second phase into action	
Survey the results after three months and make changes where required	
Feed outcomes into strategic planning for the next academic year	
Communicate, communicate and communicate the results internally	
Look for good news stories, communicate them to parents and the community, and through websites and local media	
Collaborate with other education settings to grow wellbeing as part of a healthy organisation	

© **Domini Bingham, 2011**

- empowering of individuals
- attention to the culture of the environment and commitment to a vision
- development of a coaching culture
- celebration of success.

This is what it looks like when a secondary school in the UK is practising an action wellbeing plan. When getting a wellbeing programme off the ground, always consider what you are going to include in any wellbeing action plan; the point you are starting from; what you have done; what you intend to do; and how it will be measured.

Table 2.4 *An action wellbeing plan in practice*

Action	Lead names	Resources	When	Done	Measurement
Half-termly wellbeing meetings to be set up and wellbeing team members notified		Time during working parties meeting	4/10		Meetings taken place
Suggestions made at action plan meeting to be taken to SLT meeting			7/09		Monitoring of suggestions carried out
Wellbeing to be added to agenda of faculty meetings, discussed at policy group meeting		Time during meeting			Levels of participation Satisfaction Attendance
Departments/faculties to host cake evenings to encourage cross-department socialising/networking					
Wellbeing notice board set up in main staffroom. Smaller boards to be put up around school for easy access		Paper/card/printing			Feedback survey on usefulness and reading of board
Regular pub event to take place straight after school on a Friday Everyone is encouraged to attend		Coordination of event champions to support and encourage			Usefulness Attendance Satisfaction
Wellbeing to be added to staff bulletin weekly		Wellbeing tips/events			Usefulness Attendance Satisfaction
Preparation for second staff survey on 1/11 Staff list to be printed and codes prepared		Wellbeing website materials			
Training for staff on how to complete questionnaire on 1/11 or 2/11					
Social events to be organised	Various – anyone can get involved!				Attendance Satisfaction

(Adapted courtesy of Ruislip High School)

7. Meeting in groups to discuss an action plan

How can you adapt this grid to suit your context, indicating where you are, what you have done, what you plan to do and how it will be measured?

Questions for reflection

- What is understood by the word wellbeing by staff in school settings?
- How do teachers think of their wellbeing in school? And how does it affect their approach to students?

The National College/TDA (2010) (page 2) concluded that 'successful schools define success not only in terms of test and examination results, but also in terms of personal and social outcomes, pupil and staff motivation, engagement and wellbeing, the quality of teaching and learning and the school's contribution to the community'. Does this reflect your school and if not what do you need to do?

Evaluation: What might you evaluate?

Examples of key outcomes and benefits which can be evaluated are:

- Staff report they are coping better with change.
- Staff report they are experiencing improved emotional wellbeing.
- Management report improved retention for the whole workforce.
- Management report a reduction in days lost to sickness.
- There is a reduction in the use of contract staff.
- There is improved performance impacting on pupil outcomes.

Sustaining wellbeing

Health and wellbeing champions

Introducing health and wellbeing champions and advocates throughout your organisation will help to ensure any initiatives will move forward and can be sustained.

8. Create a team of wellbeing champions across the organisation to represent all staff and sectors

- If multi-site, appoint champions from each building.
- Consider that on small sites the job role may be shared between staff with different job roles.

The importance of resilience and self-care

If, as Wiliam (2010) suggests, human beings are the most important resource, creating sustainable people becomes a critical issue. And so does creating leaders who are resilient – that is those who are able to sustain energy and effectiveness in the most challenging education environments. These skills and behaviours have been found in research undertaken by the National College to be present in leaders who show resilience:

Have self-awareness, of situations, environments and triggers that induce stress

Are able to remove or side-step causes of trigger situations

Keep outside external interests

Have external support for unloading feelings and concerns

Have strategies for holding one's temper in immediate crisis

Focus on a few long-term goals and priorities

Realise that finding an 80 per cent solution to a problem is sometimes enough

Have measurable standards, therefore knowing the job has been done and so can switch off

Are able to put problems into perspective.

(National College, 2010, page 2)

Questions for reflection

- What does a resilient leader look like?
- What do resilient staff look like?
- How do you show human beings are your most important resource?

Communicating your successes

Case study: Adopting healthier lifestyles

A primary school in the UK wanted to communicate to its internal and external stakeholders how they had been encouraging staff to adopt healthier lifestyles by being more active in their daily routines. For two

(Continued)

(Continued)

terms, all staff were encouraged to wear pedometers and keep a measurement of how many steps they walked over the course of a week. As part of this, they were encouraged to leave their cars at home, and walk to school if they lived locally or cycle to work or get off the bus one stop earlier. At the end of the two terms, 86 per cent of staff reported increased feelings of wellbeing, better sleeping patterns and reduced feelings of stress. Plans are now afoot for the children to follow the lead taken by staff. These feel-good results were shown on the school website and in the school newsletter, discussed at meetings and adopted as part of the school improvement strategy.

Helping to build on your setting's success is very important in showing your staff that you take wellbeing seriously. Once you have achieved some measurable health and wellbeing outcomes, you might wish to share your success with the educational community and more widely. In telling your story, a useful framework in building up communication is the following:

What needs did we identify?

What outcomes did we focus on?

What activities/interventions did we put in place?

What did we achieve, and how did we know?

What will we do next?

How will we communicate our success?

(Healthy Schools Toolkit, *DfE, 2011*)

Conclusion

The pressure on educational organisations will continue to increase given the emphasis on standards in UK schools and other parts of the world, so less stress on testing is unlikely. Therefore, we need to think about and provide imaginative solutions to reconceptualise the status quo for the workforce. Keeping values in times of pressure is crucial. Culture and trust play a crucial role in creating a climate for successful change. For staff, there will always be someone else to step into your shoes if you resign. From the leadership perspective, being able to cope, or having resilience, is paramount. With many of the 'Baby Boom' generation heading for retirement, the issue of succession in schools and other educational organisations and succession planning has reached critical proportions, and putting into place strategies for the wellbeing of the organisation's most precious commodity not only helps retention but makes good business sense.

> ## Questions for further thinking
>
> - What do you see as the major issues around wellbeing in your organisation?
> - How would you engage senior leadership in the wellbeing agenda?
> - How would you measure wellbeing at the start? What baseline metrics can you draw on?

Resources and useful further reading

Bubb, S. and Earley, P. (2004) *Managing Teacher Workload*. London: Paul Chapman Publishing.

Bubb, S. and Earley, P. (2010) *Helping Staff Develop in Schools*. London: Sage.

Covey, S.M.R. (2006) *The Speed of Trust*. London: Pocket Books – includes a very useful chapter on achieving organisational trust.

Goleman, D. (2007) *Social Intelligence: The New Science of Human Relationships*. London: Arrow Books – discusses the use of emotional intelligence in the workplace.

Harris, B. (2007) *Supporting the Emotional Work of School Leaders*. London: Paul Chapman Publishing.

Hartle, F., Stein, J. and Hobby, R. with O'Sullivan, M. (2007) *Retaining School Leaders*. Nottingham: National College.

Health and Safety Executive (HSE) – www.hse.gov.uk – HSE's job is to protect people against risks to health or safety arising out of work activities. Provides advice, guidance and information on inspections and regulations.

Teacher Support Network (TSN) – www.teachersupport.info/

Webb, L. (2009) *How to Work Wonders*. Grosvenor House Publishing – gives top tips for wellbeing Guildford: Grosvenor House Publishing.

Worklife Support – www.worklifesupport.com – provides wellbeing programme information and initiatives for teachers.

References

Bangs, J. (2011) In the End, Teachers are on their Own. Presentation given at the IOE.

Barber, M., Whelan, F. and Clark, M. (2010) *Capturing the Leadership Premium*. London: McKinsey & Co.

Covey, S.M.R (2006) *The Speed of Trust*. London: Pocket Books.

Crawford, M. (2009) *The Heart of Leadership*. London: Sage.

Department for Education (DfE) (2011) *Healthy Schools Toolkit*, London: DfE www.education.gov.uk/

Gold, A. (2004) *Values and Leadership*. London: Institute of Education.

Health and Safety Executive (HSE) (2003) *Managing Work Related Stress: A Guide for Managers and Teachers in Schools*. London: HSE National College.

National College (2010) *10 Strong Claims about Successful School Leadership*. Nottingham: NCSL.

National College (NCSL)/TDA (2010) *School Improvement Planning Framework 2009/10*. Nottingham: NCSL.

NCSL (2009) *Collaborative Leadership in Extended Schools*. Nottingham: NCSL.

PricewaterhouseCoopers (PWC) (2007) *Independent Study into School Leadership: Main Report*. London, DfES.

Wiliam, D. (2010) Teacher Quality: Why it Matters and How to Get More Of It. Spectator Schools Revolution Conference, March.

Conflict Resolution

Linda Trapnell

In this chapter, we will consider the following:

- Causes of conflict
- EQ, IQ and SQ intelligences
- Motivational/thinking style differences
- Approaches to analysing/preventing conflict situations
- Managing difficult conversations/holding people to account

So you've got the new job and are keen to get started. The little voice in the back of your mind is whispering unvoiced thoughts. You know that your teaching is sound and you can maintain discipline in the classroom but what about the adults you must now deal with? Where will your challenges come from?

As a leader, you will be expected to deal with a wide range of adults from members of the senior leadership team (SLT) to subject/class teachers, teaching assistants, Social Services, Psychological Services, school administrators and parents/carers. The potential for conflict echoes through the canyons of your mind as you reflect on your new post.

It may be that you know your school situation well as you had an internal promotion. You may be aware of where your challenges lie ...

It may be that there is a blank canvas awaiting you at a new school.

So where do difficult situations arise and why?

Causes of conflict

If you ask a group of leaders where they encounter conflict, the list will be long and varied. The following are nearly always included:

A clash of personalities	Ignoring the big picture
Lack of understanding	No respect from senior leaders
Issues with deadlines	Documentation issues
Gossip	Bullying by staff
Poor communication	Lack of teamwork
Resistance to change	The fact that people say 'yes' and then don't act
Different ways of working	Lack of trust

So what will you do?

First, you need to appreciate that everyone has a different way of dealing with work and with other people. It is a complex mix of their childhood experiences coupled with later life experiences and their genetic make-up.

What you can never do is change another person's behaviour if they don't want to change it themselves. What you can do is try to understand how they tick and how you can manage their behaviours to get the work done and achieve the best possible education for the students you have in your school.

EQ, IQ and SQ intelligences

One of the first things to consider is what makes YOU tick. Daniel Goleman (1995) has done extensive work on the value of emotional intelligence, especially in leaders. Leaders need to review their own capabilities with three main intelligences – IQ, EQ and SQ. The latter deals with one's ability to understand the hopes and dreams of others and society.

A good leader has a blend of all three intelligences and is aware of the impact of themselves upon others. This requires introspection on the part of the leader, and obtaining honest feedback from trusted colleagues is a valuable exercise.

A leader high in IQ (intelligence quotient) but low in the other two areas creates an individual who cannot see the impact of their actions on others and finds it difficult to establish trust.

A leader high in EQ (emotional quotient) but low in the other two areas creates an individual who is sensitive to the needs of others but can sometimes allow this to mask the needs of the organisation.

A leader high in SQ (spiritual quotient) but low in the other two areas can lead to decisions being made with high ideals but lacking awareness of impact on individuals and the organisation's needs.

Where do YOU fall and how do you know this?

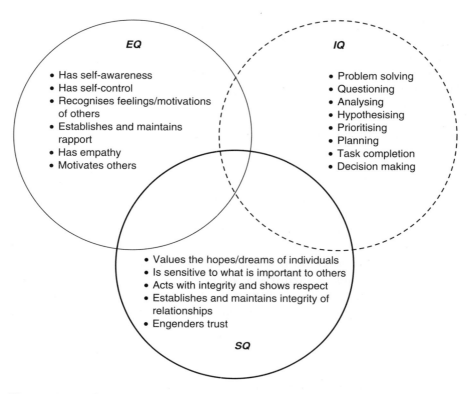

EQ
- Has self-awareness
- Has self-control
- Recognises feelings/motivations of others
- Establishes and maintains rapport
- Has empathy
- Motivates others

IQ
- Problem solving
- Questioning
- Analysing
- Hypothesising
- Prioritising
- Planning
- Task completion
- Decision making

- Values the hopes/dreams of individuals
- Is sensitive to what is important to others
- Acts with integrity and shows respect
- Establishes and maintains integrity of relationships
- Engenders trust

SQ

Figure 3.1   *IQ, EQ and SQ*

Motivational/thinking style differences

In any group of people, individuals will have widely differing motivators. A cause of conflict is often that people do not realise that this impacts on how they see the behaviour of others. The Motivational Maps® system was developed by James Sale, a recognised authority on human motivation, after five years of research in this field (www.motivationalmaps.co.uk). It provides a unique solution for managing motivation, and is based primarily on James's research into three recognised and respected sources: Maslow's Hierarchy of Needs, Edgar Schein's Career Anchors, and the Enneagram. The result is an effective and easy-to-use tool that specifically identifies what motivates people at work: www.motivationalmaps.com can provide details if you wish to complete a questionnaire to determine accurate motivators for yourself and/or your team – there is a cost.

If you look at the motivators below, three of them will probably catch your attention as being relevant to you at this moment. They will change depending on your age/home/social/work factors at any given time. One motivator may be one you don't like to see in others. This is natural, but a leader must understand that while it is not a motivator for them (or other team members) it is what drives that individual. The key is to identify these areas in you and then look at others. Do

Table 3.1   *Types of leader*

BUILDER	seeks money, material satisfactions, good standard of living
DIRECTOR	seeks power, influence, control of people/resources, decision-making responsibilities
EXPERT	seeks expertise, mastery, specialisation, knowledge
CONNECTOR	seeks belonging, friendship, fulfilling relationships
DEFENDER	seeks security, predictability, stability
STAR	seeks recognition, respect, social esteem
SEARCHER	seeks meaning, making a difference, providing worthwhile things
CREATOR	seeks innovation, identification with the new, expressing creative potential
SPIRIT	seeks freedom, independence, making own decisions, understanding of the big picture

you find someone irritating because they have different motivators? None of these motivators is 'wrong' – some just appeal to you more than others.

Conflict within teams is often the result of lack of appreciation of the motivators of the individual members. Assigning tasks and so on in line with motivators can help a team work together effectively. An example of this is that it can be counterproductive to assign a task to a 'Spirit' but then micro-manage their progress and stipulate exactly the way the task must be performed. To give them more freedom on a task with clear expectations on outcomes would probably achieve better results and produce a satisfied team member.

So, after reflection, you think you know what motivates you and the key players in your team. The way that people think and plan their work is also a factor in averting conflict when you are managing the projects/day-to-day work of your team. The research of Gregorc (1986) on the way people think/work also provides a background for managing team members. There are four main categories but obviously people can be a mix of certain types. Just by reading through the characteristics, you might begin to appreciate the issues which can arise if people have different styles yet need to work together. Often, it is enough for the team to appreciate others' differences to produce more harmonious working. It also alerts the individual to the impact of their working practices on others. A short, free questionnaire can be found online ('Gregorc Thinking Styles', at www.thelearningweb.net/personalthink.html) to use with your team to identify preferences prior to discussing the characteristics below.

Gregorc's thinking/working style characteristics

The concrete sequential individual:

- needs and enjoys structured situations
- likes to work with hands-on projects
- likes things to be ordered and arranged in specific ways
- likes clear and definite directions
- is always 'busy', looking for constructive things to do, and can't sit still for long
- is a natural organiser

- prefers to do things step by step
- follows directions
- is a natural editor – can take anything and make it better
- has a great fear of being wrong.

The abstract sequential individual:

- reads avidly for information and likes ideas presented logically
- needs a quiet environment in which to think and work
- likes to debate about ideas and controversial issues
- likes to learn just to learn – self-directed
- gathers information and analyses ideas
- strives for intellectual recognition
- thinks in a structured, logical and organised way
- fears appearing foolish or uninformed.

The abstract random individual:

- dislikes routine procedures and orderliness
- is flexible, accepting and responds easily to change
- learns well through discussions and sharing of ideas
- is imaginative
- personalises information
- is usually involved in many projects or interests
- is focused on friendships and relationships
- has a fear of not being liked.

The concrete random individual:

- is highly curious
- comes up with out-of-the-ordinary answers to problems
- seems driven to say things others have not
- is a risk-taker
- likes to discover their own way of doing things/tests things out for themselves
- is extremely independent and competitive with self
- prefers to investigate and experiment, and be hands-on
- skips steps and detail
- shows original creativity; has various ideas and thoughts
- has many projects going on at once
- finds possibilities, creates change
- is notorious for not reading instructions/directions
- fears structure.

Strategies for dealing with the various styles can be helped by this analysis.
Characteristics of the four thinking styles are given below.
As a leader, it really makes life easier if you know yourself and your team/team
members well. It is not always possible for people to work in their preferred style

Table 3.2 *The four thinking styles – individual motivators*

Type	Prefers	Possible difficulties
Concrete Sequential	Order and quiet Exact directions Guided practice Knowing the accepted way of doing things Being able to apply ideas in a practical, hands-on way Being given approval for specific work done	Making choices Open-ended tasks and 'what if' questions Dealing with opposing views Taking new approaches Interpreting abstract ideas Seeing the 'forest'
Abstract Sequential	Lectures and reading Following traditional ways Working alone Research Logical explanations Being respected for intellect	Expressing emotions openly Working co-op in groups Writing creatively Taking risks – unpredictable Open-ended problems Placing levels in perspective
Abstract Random	Co-op work Tasks with room for flexibility Balance of social activities–work Non-competitive atmosphere Personal attention/emotional support	Working alone Attending to detail and giving exact answers Working within time limits Concentrating on one task at a time Being corrected Expecting less emotional response from others
Concrete Random	A trial-and-error approach Being hands-on Brainstorming/open-ended questions Producing real creative products Original/unique approaches to problem solving Self-directed learning	Pacing and meeting time limits Completing projects Choosing one answer Keeping detailed records Prioritising Accepting another's idea without showing another view Accepting when change is impossible

but it helps if they appreciate when they are out of their comfort zone and can put extra effort into a task. In my experience, people are quick to appreciate their preferred styles and also understand why conflicts arise. A teacher commented to me: 'I now know why my classroom assistant and I don't get on – we work in different ways! We need to talk ...'

Approaches to analysing/preventing conflict situations

When the inevitable conflict does arise, it helps to try to get to the root of the problem in a logical manner (not always possible in the heat of the moment).

A good tactic is to buy time for this analysis. As a general rule:

- Calm the situation down.
- Seek time to find evidence/information.
- Show equanimity to both sides.
- Set a time to discuss issues.

The gathering of evidence/information is vital.

A 'cloud' is one of the thinking 'tools' forming the basis of the Theory of Constraints (TOC), developed by Dr E. Goldratt, philosopher/entrepreneur, to aid problem solving in industry.

His work is based on the Theory of Constraints and the techniques are recommended study in most MBA courses and degree courses for Business Studies, Production Management, etc. The novels *The Goal* (Goldratt and Cox, 1993) and *It's Not Luck* (Goldratt, 1994) were written to show how the techniques could be used in solving industrial, management and personal dilemmas.

The cloud is a diagram that describes a dilemma/conflict in a fair and non-provocative way by focusing on five questions. Any issues change focus from 'you against me' to 'us against the problem'.

First, one should consider the 'wants' of both sides in the conflict. This is usually the obvious thing in dispute. Then look at the 'needs' of both sides. What is the underlying emotional need? Then it is necessary to consider the 'common objective' of both sides in the conflict. What do they agree on?

If you are trying to analyse a problem that you are involved in, you may come to realise that while you understand your own side of a cloud, the other side is unknown to you. This then requires you to speak to the other person involved, asking relevant questions.

The cloud can be used with adults, and with students as young as 5 years old. It can be used to analyse an issue between two people or it can be used to decide upon the way forward with a personal decision where there are alternatives or there is an internal conflict.

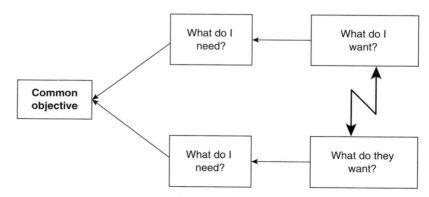

Figure 3.2

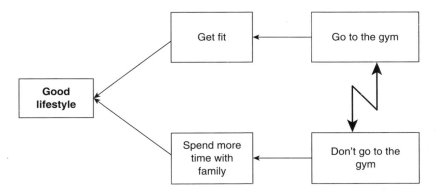

Figure 3.3

In order to have a healthy body and a good lifestyle, I should get fit and the only way to do this is to go to the gym. **An assumption has been made** …

On the other side

The only way I can have a good lifestyle is to spend more time with my family, therefore I can't go to the gym. **Another assumption has been made** …

The next step is to try to prove some of the assumptions false.

- I could take the family to the gym?
- We can exercise in other places as a family?

Two possible solutions

If you practise on 'internal' problems, it makes it easier when you tackle an interpersonal problem.

The Wants should be as near possible opposites – do/don't, can/can't, want/don't want.

The Needs will be emotionally 'deeper'.

You may need to give up your want to achieve your need.

You might want to look at some examples of clouds in many languages done by students across the world. Go to www.tocforeducation.com. This technique can be used by students and adults and is adopted by many industries as a conflict resolution tool.

Managing difficult conversations/holding people to account

Many people shy away from having a difficult conversation. You may have an issue that you must raise with a colleague/parent and you have researched the background and are aware of some of the issues/personalities you are dealing with. How do you conduct the conversation that must follow? It is helpful to structure your conversation in advance. The following guidelines should be helpful:

- Name the issue.
- Give one specific example to illustrate the issue.
- State how you feel.
- Say what you feel is at stake.
- State why you are involved.
- Say that 'We need to resolve this'.
- Invite the views of the other person.
- Don't defend or argue – just listen.

An illustration of this is when a classroom assistant has a pattern of being late for the start of a lesson, delaying the start of learning for some groups. The conversation might take the form ...

- I need to talk about your punctuality for the start of lessons.
- You were 10 minutes late into the classroom yesterday (have further evidence available).
- This is causing me problems in organising the start of learning and increasing the pressure on me.
- I feel the students are not given the best start to the day.
- It is my responsibility to ensure you fulfil your tasks in line with your job description.
- We need to resolve this.
- Can you tell me why this is happening?
- Then listen and interact.

This is also a useful format to have when dealing with parents.

There is no substitute for practice.

The book *Fierce Conversations* by Susan Scott is useful further reading around this subject (2002).

Conclusion

Conflict is, in many ways, inevitable in modern-day life but it can be dealt with intelligently by reflecting on the personalities involved and the background to events. As a leader, you will have to deal with people who strongly disagree with you and also with conflict between staff members. You will certainly need to hold people to account. I hope that the techniques outlined in this chapter will help you in your work.

Questions for further thinking

- What issues do you need to deal with in your personal life?
- What issues do you need to deal with in your professional life?
- What stops you from dealing with these issues?

Resources and useful further reading

- www.motivationalmaps.com – gives you some good basic information on motivation.
- www.thelearningweb.net/personalthink.html – allows you to find out about your own thinking style on this site.
- www.tocforeducation.com – provides plenty of examples of 'clouds' and other useful tools.
- Susan Scott (2002) *Fierce Conversations*, Berkley Trade – a very practical book with excellent advice on how to have those difficult conversations.

References

Goldratt, E. (1994) *It's not Luck*. Aldershot: Gower Press.
Goldratt, E. and Cox, J. (1993) *The Goal*, 2nd edition. Aldershot: Gower.
Goleman, D. (1995) *Emotional Intelligence*. London: Bloomsbury.
Gregorc, A. F. (1986) *An Adult's Guide to Style*. New York: Gabriel Syst.
Scott, S. (2002) *Fierce Conversations*. New York: Berkley Trade.

4

Leading Professional Learning and Development

Carol Taylor

In this chapter, we will consider the following:

- Professional development – its purpose, context and benefits
- Strategically leading professional learning and development
- Knowing what difference professional development is making
- The nine factors underpinning effective professional development
- Collaborative enquiry and coaching to support effective professional development
- Sharing and celebrating new learning and effective practice within your team

Professional development – its purpose, context and benefits

There are many definitions of professional development (PD), or continuing professional development, but a recent definition by Earley and Porritt (2010) captures what matters by saying PD is about:

> *the learning and development of the school workforce, ultimately for the purpose of enhancing the quality of education for the school's children and young people. (p. 4)*

We would all agree that the learning and development of our colleagues is vitally important for a number of reasons – but the key purpose of engaging in it is to make a positive difference to our pupils. Throughout this chapter, it may be helpful to keep this principle in mind as we explore some of the key aspects of professional learning and development.

An overview of the current context

The role of the person with overall responsibility for professional learning and professional development (PD) in organizations has been changing significantly over the last decade. The role has shifted from being mostly an administrative one to one that is more strategic – and from leading alone to where the leadership is distributed throughout the whole organization. You may be someone who has a formal title as a leader of PD or you may be leading an aspect of learning, or a phase or team, but do not have a formal title for PD. However, everyone who is responsible for leading and developing colleagues can be making a significant difference to the culture of the organization. If everyone is learning, then the organization has a greater capacity to perform well.

Those with middle leadership responsibility in schools have been pivotal in making this shift in culture. In England, the Ofsted report (2010) on effective leadership of professional development was very clear – that in the best organizations middle leaders had a key role to play.

We also now know much more about what professional development and learning opportunities are most likely to be effective. We certainly know that judicious use of external expertise is appropriate and that in many organizations and teams there is already a huge amount of expertise that can be drawn upon – but that we perhaps don't always know where this is and so are not maximizing on what is a readily accessible resource. Adults learning together in collaboration is also now recognized as being an important feature of effective PD.

Teacher learning and classroom practice are inextricably linked to school improvement. Pupil chances are improved when teachers and adults are highly effective and when the learning and teaching is appropriate and of the highest quality. It goes without saying, therefore, that the professional development of everyone in the organization should be of the highest priority.

Activity 1

This activity will help you to identify and clarify the purpose and benefits of professional development.
Discuss with your staff or your team:

- What is the purpose of professional development?
- What have been, for you, the benefits of engaging in professional learning and development?

© LCLL, 2008

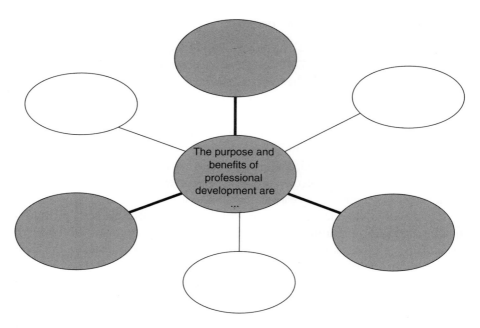

Figure 4.1

There are many acknowledged benefits of engaging in professional development. You may have come up with some of these. Using the above diagram, fill in the ones that are relevant to you:

- updating and extending knowledge and skills
- learning about new initiatives, developments or strategies
- developing competences with a view to professional career targets
- developing satisfaction, self-confidence and gaining a sense of being valued
- enabling enhancement of qualifications
- making a difference for pupils.

Case study 1: Do you know what staff think about PD?

In this large secondary school in north London, the PD leader, who was quite new to the role, wanted to ascertain what his administrative colleagues in the school felt about the value of professional development. Anecdotally, he was hearing that it was not valued and that 'little is being done to develop us'. Indeed, some staff were very negative about its value at all and others appeared to have a 'very narrow view of what professional development was'. He realized that he 'firstly needed to fully understand the extent and nature of the team's negative perceptions before secondly thinking about how to improve its understanding of what CPD is'. He therefore set up a series of questionnaires and interviews to establish exactly what the staff felt.

The results were helpful in giving him a true picture of the baseline from which he needed to build. Some staff felt that PD is about going on courses:

> the team's essentially passive view of CPD as 'being sent on courses' has led to their not recognizing the many learning experiences which do occur and which do lead to quantifiable improvements in skills and knowledge.

In conducting the questionnaires and interviews, this PD leader also began to realize that there was a lack of consistency in how PD needs were identified and further exploration revealed that there was no common system for doing this across the organization. Consequently, colleagues were getting very different experiences of the identification of their needs. This went some way to helping him to understand why colleagues felt their needs were not being met and why they felt negative about any PD they had actually experienced. It often simply did not meet their needs or the needs of the organization. This resulted in 'a loss of faith in the system and confusion about the purpose of PD'.

This PD leader did re-write the pro forma for applying for PD but at the same time noted:

> I was aware of the risk of merely devising a good system for needs identification, and so missing the real point of human resource development; the chance to involve them in a shared vision of a professional learning community which inspires them to improve their performance for a common goal.

He went on to spend half of a staff development day exploring with everyone in the organization 'PD – why should we bother?' as a way to begin to engage colleagues in vision and purpose.

Questions for reflection

- What does everyone in your organization or team agree to be the purpose and the benefits of professional development?
- What are the benefits of everyone having a common understanding of this?

Strategically leading professional learning and development

Have you taken the time to consider who or what you are leading?

As a leader of professional development, you will recognize that it is your responsibility to support and develop your colleagues and in doing that you will be more likely to create a high performing team that makes a difference to pupil outcomes.

The values and beliefs that you hold and then model will be vital in setting the tone for your team. If your colleagues see and hear you talking about learning, engaging in your own learning and so leading by example, then they will aspire to mirror these values and beliefs.

The most important message here is to be aware that while you may have other leadership responsibilities in your school, the most important aspect of your leadership is in leading people – for it is your colleagues who will support you in achieving all that you want to achieve for the pupils in your organization.

Do you have a vision for what you want your organization or team to be achieving and does your vision include everyone learning in order to achieve the agreed goals?

Effective leaders know where they are going and, crucially, so does everyone in the organization or team – the vision is created together and shared together.

Activity 2

This activity will help you to create a shared vision for professional learning and development.

You can do this activity with everyone in your organization or team.

What will they be doing?	What will they be thinking?	What will they be feeling?
What will they be achieving?	What will they be saying?	What will they be hearing?

Figure 4.2

© LCLL, 2008

You can consider what other leaders of PD say about purpose and vision on the National College website: Strategic Leadership of CPD module (www.nationalcollege.org.uk/index/professionaldevelopment/leadershippathways/leadershippathways-cpd.htm).

Those who are leading professional development strategically will align the organizational priorities with performance management and professional development.

A key question to ask here is 'is performance management seen as a judgmental process or a developmental opportunity in your organization?' In many learning organizations, performance management is called something else that better reflects its purpose. 'Learning and Development Review' or 'Professional Review' are titles that some have adopted when they want the message to be loud and clear about why they are investing huge amounts of time in the process … it's about learning and development and, implicitly then, it's about making a difference to adult learning so that it impacts on pupil learning.

Activity 3

Handscomb (2007: 87–88) identify the characteristics of an effective learning community as being one 'where research and enquiry would permeate all aspects of its life …' and goes on to cite the research of Sharpe et al. (2006) who identify the key cultural and professional development conditions for becoming a research-engaged school:

- a culture that values openness, reflection and professional debate;
- a commitment to using evidence for school improvement;
- a commitment of resources to the project;
- access to sources of expertise and support;
- a desire for people to work collaboratively, regardless of role or status;
- a willingness to embed research activity into existing systems such as staff development activities.

You could discuss each of these characteristics individually or with colleagues and consider:

- Which of these apply to your own organization and/or which apply to your team?

Now think about your own school or team as a learning community and identify:

- one thing that you could do that would build on the good practice already happening;
- one thing that you could do to improve the learning community.

While effective organizations are linking their improvement plan with performance management and with professional development, this doesn't mean that the only PD that is happening is that related to performance management. Of course, there will be lots of other professional development that is happening to support individuals but a key aspect of your role is to support the organization improvement priorities and to help your colleagues also do that – and the performance management process is a key way to make that happen.

It is also worth considering if team performance management objectives can help to make the most of the investment being made. Overarching themes that sit under the main themes in the improvement plan can be agreed across the team – with individual objectives sitting beneath that and being personalized to the individual. This can help teams to pool their knowledge and expertise and focus on making a difference to an identified group of pupils. A further bonus can come from the fact that colleagues share an invested interest – talking about common issues and sharing practice together. Equally, this can change what might have been, until this point, team meetings that have been too focused on administrative issues to meetings that focus on learning and teaching.

Questions for reflection

- How is performance management considered in your organization – as a developmental or judgmental process?
- What would need to change to make it more developmental?
- What would be the benefits and challenges if colleagues shared and owned team objectives that linked to the school improvement plan and then to their own individual objectives?

Effective leaders know where the expertise is in the organization and team. Knowing this means that they are able to call on it at the appropriate time and so give individuals the opportunity to shine. In this way, it can help to build capacity within and across the organization. Equally, if you know where the areas for development are, you can try to match the support from within the team.

Activity 4

This activity will ask you to consider and identify where the expertise is in either your organization or your team.

Table 4.1 *Identifying the expertise in your organization/team*

Questions to ask	Your responses
What strengths and expertise is already in the organization/team?	
What are you already doing as an organization/team that is working well?	
Can you/do you need to do more of it and, if so, what steps do you need to take?	
Is this working for everyone in the organization/team?	
Who needs further support?	
What might that look like?	
Where might you find this support – in the organization/team or beyond the organization/team?	

Questions for reflection

- What are the benefits of knowing where the expertise is in the organization or team?
- What are the implications of knowing this?

If the expertise is not within your team:

- Where can you find it within the organization?
- Who can you call upon to help you with this?

Knowing what difference professional development is making

Sometimes colleagues move too quickly to engage in professional development activities before being clear about:

- what difference they want to make
- to whom they want to make a difference
- by when they want to make a difference
- how they will know they've made a difference.

As a leader of professional development, you need to have absolute clarity about what it is you want to achieve before any PD activity begins:

- What difference do you want the professional development opportunity to make?

- What will be happening, and what will people be doing, achieving and feeling, when they are successful?

© LCLL, 2008

Without this clarity, you will find it difficult to know when you have achieved your goal. Often we hear colleagues say that they do have this clarity: 'I want to be a more effective leader as a result of engaging in this programme so that my team collaborate more with each other' but when pushed on what 'more effective' and 'collaborate more with each other' looks like, they are not really clear at all! Effective leaders are very clear. How clear are you about the difference that the PD engaged in is making to the adult practice and then to pupil learning and outcomes?

Are you asking the right questions before agreeing to any PD for your team or individuals? Your colleagues may find it challenging to have to answer some of these questions but if they understand the shared vision and the purpose of PD, then they are more likely to understand why you are asking them. Knowing what needs to change, what is currently happening and what you want to see happening in the future will help you, with your colleagues, to decide on the best way to achieve it – in other words, the most appropriate strategy or PD opportunity to meet the need (© LCLL, 2008).

Activity 5

As a leader, therefore, you will need to negotiate through the process carefully and sensitively and ask and be able to answer the following key questions in order to establish at the outset the difference that you want the PD to make.

First, try asking these questions of yourself in relation to some aspect of your own teaching, or your leadership, that you wish to make a difference to:

Table 4.2 *Making a difference in your teaching or leadership*

Questions to ask	Your responses
What difference do you/your team/your colleague want to make?	
For which pupils?	
What is happening now for you, your team, this colleague and these pupils?	
How do you know?	
What is working well that you can build on?	
What needs to change if you are to be successful?	
By when will you aim to achieve the change?	

Questions to ask	Your responses
How will you know that the change has made a positive difference?	
What will you be looking for?	
What evidence of the change will you need? What evidence do you trust?	
What support/PD will you need to achieve this change?	

Every individual in your team will learn in different ways and a professional development opportunity that works for one person may not be the best professional development opportunity for another. Just as your pupils have preferred learning styles, so too do adults.

Questions for reflection

- How are the needs of pupils central to decisions currently made about professional development?
- Are you having rigorous discussions about the difference that you want the professional development to make?
- Are those discussions establishing at the very start what difference will be seen, to whom and by when – and how you will know?
- How will the impact of the professional development, changes in practice and pupil learning be monitored over time? By whom?
- What do you need to change as a leader in the way PD is agreed for your team?

What professional development is likely to make the most difference?

Simply put, the answer here is whatever professional development opportunities make the most difference to the adult and then to the pupils.

As we have already said, your colleagues will learn in different ways and there is no one PD activity that is top of the list. However, we know a lot about what professional development opportunities have the potential to make the most impact – but whatever is agreed between you and a colleague it must meet their preferred need, it must be of high quality and it must be fit for purpose. So, if subject knowledge development is what is needed then attending a one day external course isn't probably going to meet that need. The need would be better met using internal and ongoing expertise from within the team.

Changing teacher practice is very difficult – it's hard to change what teach-ers do every day and we need to be cognizant of this and not expect change to happen over-night. How many times have you engaged in a professional learning opportunity and been inspired and motivated but then gone back to your job and almost forgotten about it? Why is that? Well, often it is because there is no ongoing support – through coaching or otherwise – to help you identify what it is you need and can do and then for that support to be ongoing. There are some interesting case studies that will be helpful to you in setting up coaching on your organization on both the National College website and in the Earley and Porritt (2010) publication.

Activity 6

This activity will help you to identify and agree the common elements of effective professional development.
   You can discuss these questions with a group of colleagues.

Table 4.3 *Identifying the common elements of effective professional development (PD)*

1. Think of a PD activity that you experienced that made a positive difference to you and your pupils.
2. What made this experience effective for you?
3. What was the difference you made as a result of this PD?
4. How do you know that it made a difference? What evidence do you have?

The nine factors underpinning effective professional development

In their book *Effective Practices in Continuing Professional Development*, Earley and Porritt (2010) identified nine factors that underpin effective professional development.

Activity 7

This activity will help you identify where there is already effective prac-tice happening around professional development and help to highlight possible areas for you to focus on. You can complete this activity, either with your organization or a specific team that you are leading in mind.

Consider what happens when professional development is agreed for you or by you for members of your team and respond appropriately to each scenario.

Table 4.4 *Identifying areas for professional development*

Earley and Porritt's nine factors of effective professional development (2010)	This always happens	This sometimes happens	This rarely or never happens
Colleague(s) have clarity about the purpose at the outset in any PD activity			
There is a focus on pupil outcomes in PD activity			
Colleagues have ownership of the support/professional development activity			
There is understanding of how to evaluate the impact of the PD			
The focus and goal are aligned to a clear timescale			
Collaborative approaches to PD are ensured			
Time is allocated for reflection and feedback			
There is engagement in a variety of PD activities/opportunities			
There is development of strategic leadership of PD			

© LCLL, 2010

Questions for reflection

Look at those factors that rarely/never happen in your organization or team:

- What would be the benefits if these were to happen more?
- What are the challenges in making this happen?

So far you have considered some important factors in leading the professional development of your team strategically:

- the benefits and purpose of professional development
- your role in leading the professional development of your team

(Continued)

(Continued)

- your vision for professional development in your team
- what leading professional development strategically means and
- the factors that underpin effective professional development.

Activity 8: Case study 2: How can you support?

This activity will help you to apply some of your thinking from the previous activities.
   Read the case study below and consider:

- How might you respond to this challenge?
- What professional development strategies might be appropriate in this situation?
- How can you ensure your work impacts on the teacher's practice first and then on pupil learning?

As a team leader, you have been supporting a science NQT who is growing in confidence and keen to develop her practice. However, she has a tendency to over-direct pupil activities; she relies heavily on worksheets and pupils mainly work individually. Her main areas for development are around ensuring pupils are actively engaged in their learning and that learning outcomes are sufficiently differentiated. When you discuss this with her, she is a little defensive and feels she is progressing well. She says, 'I'm pleased – at least they're all in their seats and working quietly.'
   The head is concerned about school data which shows that, over the last two years, pupil progress in science has remained static and actually declined for some groups of pupils. This is in contrast to the other core subjects where achievement is steadily improving. The head is keen to develop a programme of professional development to help the science team move forward and improve outcomes for pupils.

Questions for reflection

Whatever ideas you may have to support this colleague, now go back to Activity 7 and consider how many of the factors are reflected in your ideas to support the NQT.

- What else could you add into the response that might build the potential to make a greater difference?
- What have you not considered that you need to know more about?

Collaborative enquiry and coaching to support effective professional development

There is now much evidence to suggest that enquiry-based classroom research has the potential to make a difference to the adults' practice and so to pupil outcomes. This is probably because teachers are clear about what they want to make a difference to and for which pupils, and so are highly motivated to succeed.

It is also based on the premise that teachers are continually asking questions about their everyday practice.

A typical cycle includes:

- teachers/adults reflecting on their own practice
- identifying an issue
- auditing and reflecting on what is already happening
- planning the enquiry/development work
- analysing/interpreting emerging evidence
- implementing the action suggested
- reviewing the impact
- planning the next steps.

It involves colleagues:

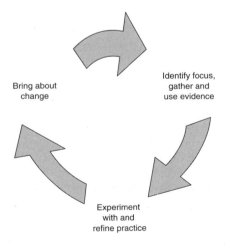

Bring about change

Identify focus, gather and use evidence

Experiment with and refine practice

Figure 4.3

(Continued)

(Continued)

- learning from research approaches
- being rigorous
- having a clear focus on impact
- identifying the evidence base
- supporting and being supported through coaching
- bringing about change
- consolidating existing skills and developing new ones
- sharing their findings with others.
© LCLL, 2008

Earley and Porritt (2010) identified collaboration as potentially extremely powerful in creating a supportive network of people with a common focus and a range of expertise and resources that can be shared. There is now a greater understanding of the potential for collaborative enquiry to make a difference to adult learning and so to pupil learning.

We know that adults welcome opportunities to plan, exchange knowledge and share expertise within a supportive community. Such an approach can help colleagues to really unpick and understand their tacit knowledge and, by sharing and discussing with others, make this more explicit.

Collaboration also helps to create collegiality and confidence and so also impacts on the general wellbeing of colleagues.

Collaborative groups can be created internally from parties interested in engaging in similar issues; from external groups or a mixture of both. In the first instance, as with many aspects of new practice, starting small is probably advisable and so creating opportunities for collaboration within your team can be a good place to start.

Before you begin any collaborative project, it will be important to have clarity about:

- the purpose of collaborating
- what it is you want to achieve and the difference you want to make
- how the work will be monitored
- how the group will be organized
- the timescale of the project/focus
- how often you will meet formally to share, discuss and agree next steps
- what other support you might need and from whom – can the senior leadership help with time, observations, resources?

Eventually you and your team might wish to share what you are learning with colleagues across the organization – but don't agree to do this until you have something worth sharing! Colleagues may be very interested in what you are doing but what is most important to also share is the difference that it is making and – of course – how you know!

When coaching is also put into this collaborative enquiry mix, there is even greater potential for both collaboration and impact as colleagues.

Activity 9

Identify with a group of colleagues a project, issue or question that you have been wanting your team to focus on.

Look at the enquiry cycle above and what is involved and identify what you would need to do to set up a collaborative enquiry.

How coaching can help to maximize any professional development opportunity

Coaching to support professional learning and development can be a highly effective approach. It can enable colleagues to move from where they currently are to where they want to be. It is probably true to say that it is about helping someone to learn rather than about telling or teaching them – so engendering a sense of ownership about what they are doing and how they are going to do it.

Coaching involves:

- raising awareness and encouraging responsibility
- listening and questioning to enable understanding
- supporting the coachee to identify what is important/relevant to them
- enabling the coachee to understand him/herself and their context more fully
- helping the coachee to understand and articulate what they want for the future and what will motivate them
- exploring options with the coachee
- agreeing actions and support.

Coaching is a skill that requires understanding and practice and is a strategy that any team can adopt. It is a myth to say 'we don't have time for coaching conversations' as there is a spectrum of coaching – it can be a loose and informal response to a situation, for example 'What options do you feel you have?' or 'What is going to be key to your success with that?', to one-to-one coaching sessions that are timed and have an agreed agenda. There are also benefits to leading group coaching sessions that can help the team agree key objectives or priorities or explore possible options and ways forward.

Again, if you look back to the characteristics of effective professional development and the nine factors identified by Earley and Porritt (2010) and consider coaching as an approach to support, you will see that it can hit many of their characteristics.

> ## Questions for reflection
>
> - How would a coaching approach help colleagues before, during and after any professional development activity?
> - Who in your organization/team already has coaching experience that you can build on?
> - Is there someone in your team who might embrace the opportunity to develop their coaching skills?

Sharing and celebrating new learning and effective practice within your team

As a leader, you can be more effective if, once you know what is working well and where it is working well, you can share it with others in the team and so build greater capacity across the team and even across the organization. If you are clear about what practice is making a difference, what the difference is and how you know then your colleagues will want to hear about it – and it's an opportunity for celebrating success!

A key challenge for all leaders is how to develop structures and systems for sharing learning and effective practice. So often, individual expertise is developed but when the individual leaves the organization their learning goes with them. As we have seen, collaborative classroom-based enquiry can also create a structure for sharing expertise within and across the team – and eventually, even across the organization through teacher learning communities.

We often hear colleagues talking about sharing learning but, as we hopefully now understand, if we want to make a difference in classrooms then simply sharing is not enough. To support change requires much more – but it is not the sole job of the formal leader to make this happen. As we have already said, knowing where the expertise is in your team means that you can offer colleagues the opportunity to lead on areas or projects that interest them or where they have the skills and expertise to lead. Distributing leadership throughout the team can build capacity and sustainability and create time for yourself to be a more effective and strategic leader.

Conclusion

Finally, is the professional development opportunity cost-effective? While this is placed here as a last question, it is not to be forgotten! However, I would suggest that the question can only be answered if we go back to the very beginning and ask the question 'What difference do we want to make, to whom and by when?' If we can answer these questions, we can then decide if, having costed out the time, resources, support and ongoing development associated with any professional development opportunity, these costs are worth it to our organization and its vision and goals.

Questions for further thinking

- What could you do to ensure that effective professional development and learning are effectively shared across the team and then the organization so that a difference is made first to adult practice and then to pupil learning?
- How could collaborative enquiry help you to share effective practice and to become a stronger learning community?
- What else could you do as an organization or team to celebrate the success of individuals in it?

Resources and useful further reading

Earley, P. and Porritt, V. (2010) *Effective Practices in Continuing Professional Development: Lessons from Schools.* London: Institute of Education Publications – provides plenty of examples of good practice and case studies from schools.

National College (NCSL) (2010) Strategic Leadership of CPD module. Available at: www.nationalcollege.org.uk/index/professionaldevelopment/leadershippathways/leadershippathways-cpd.htm – leads you through the strategic leadership of CPD.

References

Bubb, S. and Earley, P. (2007) *Leading and Managing Continuing Professional Development.* London: Paul Chapman/Sage.

Earley, P. and Porritt, V. (2010) *Effective Practices in Continuing Professional Development: Lessons from Schools.* London: Institute of Education Publications.

Handscomb, G. (2007) Collaboration and Enquiry: Sharing practice, in S. Bubb, and P. Earley *Leading and Managing Continuing Professional Development*, 2nd edition, pp. 87–88. London: Sage.

London Centre for Leadership in Learning (LCLL) (2008) *Innovative Leadership of Professional Development Programme.* London: Institute of Education Publications.

London Centre for Leadership in Learning (LCLL) (2010) *Innovative Leadership of Professional Development Programme.* London: Institute of Education Publications.

National College (NCSL) (2010) Strategic Leadership of CPD module. Available at: www.nationalcollege.org.uk/index/professionaldevelopment/leadershippathways/leadershippathways-cpd.htm

Office for Standards in Education (Ofsted) (2010) *Good Professional Development in Schools: How Does Leadership Contribute?* London: Ofsted.

Sharpe, C., Eames, A., Saunders, D. and Thomlinson, K. (2006) *Postcards from Research Engaged Schools.* Slough: NFER.

Leading Support Staff

Pauline Lyons

In this chapter, we will consider the following:

- The importance of both leading and managing
- Case study: St John's primary school
- A career development framework for staff development for all members of staff
- A leadership programme to develop the leadership and management of support staff by support staff
- Psychological theories

Leading and managing a school is one of the most privileged jobs in the world.

In this chapter, I am going to tell the story of one school that has successfully distributed the leadership and management of support staff by support staff.

The importance of both leading and managing

Leading and managing go hand in hand. They are two sides of the same coin. Strong leadership has to be combined with strong management and it has to be in balance. John Kotter (2001) says that leaders prepare organisations for change and help them cope as they make that change. Management is about coping with the complexity that that change brings. A school must be *equally* led and managed.

The story that you are about to read is of a school – I shall call it St John's, a primary school in London.

Case study: St John's Primary School

The historical context

To give you the historical context, in 2003 when the story begins, there were major changes made at a national level. The National Agreement (September 2003) introduced a series of significant changes to teachers' conditions of service. It also acknowledged the role played by support staff in schools. The Higher Level Teaching Assistant Standards (HLTA) were developed by the Training and Development Agency (TDA) and formed part of a suite of standards for teaching staff in school. Later on, the National Occupational Standards (NOS) for Teaching Assistants were revised. The National Agreement called for a change process that would enable schools to implement the contractual changes and reform the workforce.

The arrival of the new head teacher

When the new head teacher arrived at St John's in 2003, there was no senior management team. The culture of the school was one of autocratic leadership and management by the head teacher. The new head's preferred leadership style in this situation (a coaching/consultative style), together with his moral position of fairness, transparency and equality gave the impetus for a seven-year plan to change St John's staffing structures.

In 2004, the teaching staff posts were restructured. The support staff were positive towards the future implementation of restructured support staff posts in the school as they could see that, through the restructuring process, it brought openness, transparency, clarity of agreed conditions of service, standardised job descriptions, rates of pay and an entitlement to training and development.

The local authority at this time also revised the job descriptions and pay structure for the support teaching staff. This had been achieved in full consultation with the unions and gave a local framework for consistency, pay progression and career progression for support teaching staff.

Introduction of distributed leadership

One of the job descriptions had an element of management in it, together with the higher status of Higher Level Teaching Assistant (HLTA). This is a nationally recognised status that forms part of the

(Continued)

(Continued)

suite of statuses managed at that time by the Training and Development Agency (TDA). The statuses range from HLTA for support staff through newly qualified teacher to advanced skills teacher.

Thus, the development for distributed management of support staff by support staff at St John's was part of a whole-school culture change for *all* staff.

Initially, there was full consultation with all staff and the governing body. This was first done via the staffing committee and then brought to the whole governing body.

It is worth noting at this point that support staff did not perceive themselves as managers nor indeed were perceived as such by the rest of the staff.

Within the new structure, there were two posts for a HLTA, both of which included an element of staff management. The level of these posts was deemed to be middle-leader level. At that time, two members of staff completed the training for HLTA, were found competent when judged against the standards, and therefore achieved the status of HLTA. Since then, seven other members of staff have been given the opportunity to train and/or be assessed against the HLTA standards, and, for various reasons, are not yet competent. The reason for two candidates was their inadequate level of English. This knowledge has changed the practice of the school with regard to the selection of future staff. A high level of written and spoken English is now part of the selection criteria as is clarity of conditions of service (such as working hours).

The development of the new HLTA support staff to assume their management duties was carefully considered by the leadership team of the school. It was two-pronged. First, the local authority was commissioned to devise a team leading course specifically for members of the support staff who had managerial responsibilities in school. Performance management of other staff was an element of the course. Second, the school set up a three-year development plan at school for the support staff. In the first year, the HLTAs would have limited management responsibility and would be paid at the appropriate scale. During this year, the performance management of a member of the support staff would be as it usually was, i.e. an assistant head teacher (AHT) would meet with staff but for the first year this meeting and the process was *observed* by the HLTA. In the second year, the HLTA would have responsibility for the member of support staff and the *AHT* would observe. In the third year, the HLTA would take full responsibility and the AHT would act as a consultant. Therefore, the development of the HLTA was carefully managed over the long term.

This model was also mirrored in the school office as the senior administration officer conducted the performance management process of the admin staff. *Everyone's* performance in the school is managed.

The head teacher has changed the timing of his performance management so that his performance management review is first. His view that his performance management and the targets that are set should be shared with all staff resonates with his leadership style of openness. Indeed, all staff have one common target for pupil achievement and all staff are expected to be familiar with the school's plans for improvement. In addition to the common school target, there are then personal targets.

The distributed management of support staff by support staff has been part of a seven-year strategic plan. Obviously, the details of that plan were worked out on a rolling yearly plan, but the direction and vision were envisaged in 2003.

Other changes

Other things have changed as the planning and reflective process continues. One is the management of sickness, which is consistently applied. Another is that the probation period for all staff is rigorous (and is at times extended). The process is transparent. There is the possibility that a member of staff could be paired with another manager should there be a personality clash but that rarely happens.

The value system of the head teacher of fairness, openness and equality, combined with the rationale that if you do the same job you should have the same conditions of service, underpins the whole school. The values are articulated and communicated. The procedures of capability dovetail with policies such as performance management and procedures such as classroom observation.

The school has an expectation that support staff are professional people doing a professional job.

HLTAs

The head teacher has noticed a change in the applicants coming forward for teaching assistant jobs. Increasingly, there are more men applying for the job; people have higher qualifications; candidates see being a teaching assistant as a paid internship to prepare for other roles – teachers, priests, educational psychologists. St John's School's workforce reflects the ethnic diversity of the children in the school and the gender balance of men to women is changing.

(Continued)

(Continued)

I asked the head teacher what impact the course run by the local authority had had. He said that as all the staff knew that the HLTAs were going on a management course, it gave them public kudos that the school was investing in their training and that the school had an expectation that they would be managing other colleagues. The HLTAs had reflected on every session and discussed implications of ideas and thoughts back at school. The session on how to deal with difficult staff had been helpful and had had a direct impact on the way in which a particular situation was handled. The skills of people management were developed.

The HLTAs had to manage others in a fair and open way. Staff would come to them with questions. At first, they turned to their 'internal consultant' but, when given 'permission' to answer the questions of the staff, they gained the confidence to answer them directly (and as a consequence had more questions asked of them!).

The HLTAs found the new role challenging at first, but by going out of school to a 'management course' it helped them gain authority. The head teacher is very clear that people should go to the right person. There must be clear lines of communication and that must include support staff. Support staff need to be empowered to do their management job effectively with a sense of pride and enjoyment.

The head teacher noticed that when the HLTAs came back they were more confident, more articulate and more assertive. They had 'the authority of going on a course'. They met people from other school situations and reflected on their own situation and that of their colleagues in different schools.

The impact on the whole school

The school also had an inset day to reflect on the idea that everyone in school is a leader. *All* are leading at different levels. The head teacher is accountable but all are leading in different ways. The head teacher has also noticed a change in all staff with regard to management posts. There was a time when nobody applied for a management post as the collegiality in the staff room meant that people were reticent to apply for a higher post as they did not want to go up against a colleague for the job. That does not happen now. People apply and there is competition for posts. One person applied and got a job and that has now changed the culture of the school in that people want leadership and management roles.

Every year, the school sends out a letter to each member of staff with their pay scale, spine point, working hours and conditions of service. The head expects that it is every member of staff's responsibility to check the contents and to raise any queries to challenge or seek clarification. This letter is usually put in the member of staff's pigeonhole. This year, the school changed its distribution practice and the letters were posted home to staff. This change was positive. The contents of the letter were confidential to the individual and the privacy afforded by having the letter to open at home struck the right balance between openness and respect for the individual's confidential information.

The school has high standards of integrity and expects high standards of personal responsibility of its staff. As the head said, everything within school – and that includes the management of support staff by support staff – is for the benefit of the children.

Management of change

It can be clearly seen that this change was led well. There were three questions that the head teacher and the school answered. Where are we now? Where are we going? How are we going to get there? I have answered them by reference to the school's Ofsted inspection which is an external evaluation of the school in response to those three key questions:

1. Where are we now?

Answer: 'The head teacher and strong senior team have an accurate view of the school's strengths and areas that are in need of improvement. This is based on honest and discerning monitoring.'

2. Where are we going?

Answer: 'The head teacher embeds ambition and drives improvement very well. Along with senior leaders and governors he has communicated a clear vision and programme for improvement and secured the support of all.'

3. How are we going to get there?

Answer: 'The professional development of staff is very effective and ensures that they are well prepared to meet the changing needs of the

(Continued)

(Continued)

school.' Support staff are an important part of the team and work well, helping pupils in their learning.

This change is now in its eighth year and it is constantly being developed.

A career development framework for staff development for all members of staff

The career development table

Table 5.1 *The Career Development Table*

	Who is involved	Actions	Time
School needs analysis			
Recruitment			
Selection			
Induction			
Performance			
Development in role			
Success			
Transition to new role			

I find this framework useful as it lists the various steps involved in staff recruitment and development and can be used in many different scenarios yet is a consistent process.

I have filled in one as an example of whole-school leadership and management. In this example, there has been an application from a parent for a school place for a child with Down's syndrome. The staffing implications for a new member of support staff are as follows:

Table 5.2

	Who is involved	Actions	Time
School needs analysis	Local authority special educational needs panel Admissions team Governors' finance committee Governors' personnel committee	Send statement and liaise with school Assess budget implications Review support staff structure in school to evaluate whether or not a new member of staff is required	Spring term 2 Academic year 2010/11

	Who is involved	Actions	Time
Recruitment	Head teacher/personnel committee Senior Admin Officer/head teacher/governing body Educational psychologist	Write job description based on NOS Set up interview process Give advice	Summer term 1 Academic year 2010/11
Selection	Personnel committee	The best person for the job is selected	June in summer term Academic year 2010/11
Induction	Admin officer Local authority HLTA line manager Colleague SENCO	Starter forms, locker key Training and Development Agency induction programme School induction programme 'Buddy' supporter Liaise with outside agencies and parents to give knowledge of condition in general and of particular child	July in summer term Academic year 2010/11
Performance	HLTA	Performance objectives taken from TDASTL39 Support pupils with communication and interaction needs	Autumn term 2011/12
Development in role	HLTA and SENCO to arrange training	**NUMICON** training delivered by fully accredited Down's Syndrome Association training officer	Inset day October 2011
Success	1. HT 2. HLTA	1. HT to set up and carry out formal probation review meeting (briefed by HLTA line manager) 2. Performance objectives met at annual appraisal meeting	1. December 2011 2. Summer term 2012
Transition to new role	HT and HLTA	Following outcomes of annual appraisal meeting	Summer term Academic year 2011/12

A leadership programme to develop the leadership and management of support staff by support staff

The learning objectives were to develop the leadership and management skills of the HLTAs as defined in the National Occupational Standards for Supporting Teaching and Learning in Schools (NOS STL), Unit STL63: Provide Leadership for Your Team.

The National Occupational Standards for teaching assistants were developed in 2007. These standards for supporting teaching and learning in schools can be used as a starting point for designing new job roles, for developing job descriptions, for recruitment and selection, for performance management, for analysing training needs to give the structure and content of educational training, and are used as the basis for National Vocational Qualifications (NVQs) and for units in the new Qualification and Credit Framework (QCF). (They can be found on the TDA website at www.tda.gov.uk/support-staff/developing-progressing/nos/~/media/resources/support-staff/nos/slt63providing-team-leadership.pdf (accessed December 2011).)

All NOS have performance criteria (which the performance of staff can be measured against), an inventory of detailed knowledge and understanding required to do the job, and, in addition, Unit STL63: Provide Leadership for Your Team has a list of behaviours that staff must demonstrate, along with a list of skills. The skills are: communicating, planning, team building, leading by example, providing feedback, setting objectives, motivating, consulting, problem solving, valuing and supporting others, monitoring, managing conflict, decision making and following.

I wrote the course and structured it by using the words How to ... Each session was structured in the same way, which was based on Kolb's (1984) theory of learning, and each session had a small input of relevant theoretical knowledge.

I shall not discuss Goleman's emotional intelligence here as it is covered in detail in Linda Trapnell's chapter (Chapter 3).

Psychological theories

Berne's theory of transactional analysis

Eric Berne's theory (1975) of transactional analysis (TA) is based on the premise that verbal communication, particularly face to face, is at the centre of human interaction. He says that when two people encounter each other, one of them will speak to the other. This he called the Transaction Stimulus.

Table 5.3 *The leadership course*

How to ...	Theoretical input
How to communicate with your team	Berne's theory
How to manage difficult individuals	Goleman's theory of emotional intelligence
How to motivate your team	Hertzberg
	Maslow
How to do performance management	Local authority's support staff performance management system
How to develop your team	Kolb
	Learning Styles, Hay Group

The reaction from the other person he called the Transaction Response. Berne also said that each person is made up of three alter-ego states: parent, adult and child.

Parent: This is our learned voice of authority, developed from when we were young. The Parent ego state is often described as either Nurturing or Controlling.

Adult: Our 'Adult' is our rational, calm, what is often called professional state.

Child: This is our raw emotional side. Child is often described as either Adapted–Co-operative (positive) and Compliant/Resistant (negative) or Free–Spontaneous (positive) and Immature (negative).

When we communicate, we are doing so from one of our own ego states, our Parent, Adult or Child. Our feelings at the time determine which one we use, and at any time something can trigger a shift from one state to another. When we respond, we are also doing this from one of the three states. Transactional Analysis analyses this.

At the centre of Berne's theory is the rule that effective transactions (i.e. successful communications) must be complementary. Communication must go back from the receiving ego state to the sending ego state. For example, if the stimulus is Parent to Child, the response must be Child to Parent, or the transaction is 'crossed', and there will be a problem between sender and receiver. If a crossed transaction occurs, there is an ineffective communication.

In serious breakdowns, there is no chance of immediately resuming a discussion about the original subject matter. Attention is focused on the relationship. The discussion can only continue constructively when and if the relationship is mended.

One of the dangers when we are leading is to use our parent voice, the voice of authority. We should not be surprised if people respond as a child. We need to aim for adult-to-adult communication.

Herzberg's theory of motivation

Herzberg's theory of motivation (1996) states that the following will motivate us at work:

- Achievement
- Advancement
- Growth
- Recognition
- Responsibility
- The work itself

You can see from the case study how these motivated the HTAs.

Herzberg's 'hygiene factors'

Herzberg (1954) says that there are what he calls 'hygiene factors', which will negatively affect our motivation by making us dissatisfied:

- Pay
- Policy
- Security
- Status
- Supervisory style
- Working conditions

Maslow's hierarchy of needs

Abraham Maslow's (1954) hierarchy of needs also considers motivation. Maslow says we are motivated by unmet needs. Once a need is met, it is no longer a motivator:

- Self-actualisation – personal growth and fulfilment
- Esteem needs – achievement, status, reputation
- Love and affection needs – the need for belonging, for relationships
- Safety needs – security and protection
- Physiological needs – our basic need for food, water, air, etc.

We recognise this hierarchy in action when we see people in a war zone ignoring their safety needs in order to get food or water – their basic needs. As leaders, we need to consider how we are meeting the needs of our staff.

Kolb's model of learning and development

David Kolb, a psychologist, developed a model of learning and development. His 1984 book, *Experiential Learning: Experience as the Source of Learning and*

Table 5.4 *Kolb's learning grid*

	Concrete experience (CE)	
Active experimentation (AE)		Reflective observation (RO)
	Abstract conceptualisation (AC)	

Development, explains the model in detail and shows how this model of learning is based on research in psychology, philosophy and physiology.

Kolb defines learning as 'the process of creating knowledge through the transformation of experience' (1984: 38). Kolb describes four distinct underlying structures of learning: concrete experience (CE), reflective observation (RO), abstract conceptualisation (AC) and active experimentation (AE). Individuals are orientated towards different aspects of this learning grid.

> *An orientation towards concrete experience focuses on being involved in experiences and dealing with immediate human situations in a personal way. An orientation toward reflective observation focuses on understanding the meaning of ideas and situations by carefully observing and impartially describing them. An orientation towards abstract conceptualisation focuses on using logic, ideas and concepts. An orientation towards active experimentation focuses on actively influencing people and changing situations.*
> *(Kolb, 1984: 68–9)*

Learning is a complex interaction of all the aspects of learning. It is the combination of all four of the areas (CE, RO, AC, AE), which produce the highest levels of learning.

I have found this model extremely helpful in the professional development of staff in school. I use it to structure any course or learning 'event' that I devise as I choose one sector to begin with (such as a CE); we reflect on that experience (RO); we then examine possible concepts (AC); and then try them out in another situation (AE).

An example of this was when a group of support staff were learning to develop the skill of managing conflict. A member of the group gave a real example of conflict within her school that, as a manager, she was having to deal with (CE). Through group discussion, we reflected on the situation (RO) and then came up with a process for managing conflict (AC) which the members of the group then tried back in their own schools with their particular examples of conflicts that they had to manage (AE). At the next meeting, we then shared with each other the experiences that we had had (CE) and reflected on them (RO), and so on. The loop of learning never ends.

Kolb has constructed a Learning Styles Inventory (LSI) (which can be purchased at www.haygroup.com/leadershipandtalentondemand/index.aspx (accessed December 2011)).

The Learning Style Inventory is norm-referenced. There are a series of questions that are given a value. The score is then plotted on a graph. This graph gives a visualisation of the individual's pattern of orientation towards the aspects of learning (CE, RO, AC, AE). Some people are very balanced between styles, while others have a strong dominant style.

It is an excellent concrete experience to understand one's own learning style and, when used by others, that of the team. It also gives the basis for personal development. I think that to lead and manage others, you must lead and manage yourself. The LSI gives an insight into 'Where am I now?' so that from that understanding we can move to 'Where am I going?' and 'How am I going to get there?' When I did it for myself, I did not have a high score in the area of reflective observation. Since doing the LSI, I purposefully used reflective observation so that I could develop this area of learning and now I reflect all the time! As I said before, it is the combination of *all* the areas of learning that produces the highest levels of learning.

In schools, we are all leaders of learning, and the LSI is a powerful tool to enable support staff to lead the learning of staff in school.

The National Occupational Standards are underused in leading and managing support staff. In a recent report (Ofsted, 2010), a key finding was:

In all but three of the schools visited, those involved in the induction, training and management of the performance of the wider workforce did not have a secure knowledge and understanding of the national occupational standards and the career development framework because they did not know where to go for information and guidance. This delays the development of the wider workforce as a coherent, fully trained professional body.

By using the NOS to structure a leadership course, this will enable support staff to lead and manage other support staff. The performance descriptors can be used in the school's appraisal system.

Conclusion

I hope that in this chapter I have given an example of a school which is well led and managed and has carefully developed a structure and culture of management of support staff by support staff over a period of time. I wanted to show that distributed leadership and management is a planned process that has as its bedrock a positive value system of openness and fairness. The theory of experimental learning is most appropriate for adults learning in school and can be used in any situation where adults are learning, both as employees and in their personal development. Kolb's (1984) work is a shell into which any content of leadership skill development can be added. The National Occupational Standards can be used to give consistency, openness and fairness to members of the support staff, and the career development table can be used for any member of staff to clarify which development is relevant at each particular point on their career and life path. These are some tools for leadership.

Questions for further thinking

- How far has your school developed distributed leadership?
- What underpinned the success of the change process?
- Why is it important to understand how to lead support staff?
- What lessons does this case study teach you?

Resources and useful further reading

Bubb, S. and Earley, P. (2004) *Managing Teacher Workload*. Paul Chapman Publishing: London – has a good chapter on support staff.

www.haygroup.com/uk

NCSL (2004) *Distributed Leadership*. Nottingham: NCSL – is helpful in putting theory into practice.

NCSL (2005) *Leadership Development and Personal Effectiveness*. Nottingham: NCSL – provides a thought-provoking guide.

NCSL (2003) *The Heart of the Matter: A Practical Guide to What Middle Leaders can do to Improve Learning in Secondary Schools*. Nottingham: NCSL – is clearly explained.

www.ofsted.gov.uk

Robertson, J. (2008) *Coaching Educational Leadership*. London: Sage – gives some practical ideas.

Rogers, J. (2009) *Coaching Skills*. Maidenhead: Oxford University Press – provides a very practical guide to coaching.

www.tda.gov.uk

References

Berne, E. (1975) *What Do You Say After You Say Hello?* London: Corgi.

Herzberg, F. (1996) *Work and the Nature of Man*. New York: Staples Press.

Kolb, D.A. (1984) *Experiential Learning: Experience as the Source of Learning and Development*. Simon and Schuster: New York.

Kotter, J.P. (2001) *What Leaders Really Do*. Cambridge, MA: Harvard Business School Publishing Co.

Maslow, A. (1954) *Motivation and Personality*. New York: Harper and Row.

Ofsted (2010) *Workforce Reform in Schools: Has it Made a Difference?* London: Ofsted. An evaluation of changes made to the school workforce 2003–2009.

Part II

Leading and Managing within the School

6

Leading and Managing Finance[1]

Douglas MacIldowie

In this chapter, we will consider the following:

- Introduction: the whole-school perspective
- Where the money comes from: sources of funding
- Building your budget
- Monitoring expenditure
- Reporting progress
- Securing value for money
- Benchmarking
- Case study: coping with the unexpected
- Commentary on the case study

Introduction: the whole-school perspective

This chapter is broadly based on an introductory workshop I designed for aspiring head teachers on the NPQH programme. So the perspective from start to finish is of the whole-school budget and its planning and management. If you are currently leading a department or team with a more modest budget, I hope that many of the principles stated in this chapter concerning budget planning, monitoring expenditure and securing good value for money will be relevant to you. I have found when working on finance with subject leaders and pastoral staff that they are also interested in the whole-school perspective, and I hope you will be too!

[1] This chapter is based on materials initially created by Douglas MacIldowie for the London Centre for Leadership in Learning, Institute of Education.

Where the money comes from: sources of funding

As in all budgets, it's important to know where the money is coming from. This is important for two reasons: first, to ensure that the school is getting its full entitlement, and second, to be aware of what constraints may be placed on how some funds may be spent.

Table 6.1 *Sources of funding for schools*

Source	Comments
Delegated budget from the LA (including the Dedicated Schools Grant (DSG) and funding for post-16 (formerly from the VPLA))	The largest single source of income; mainly determined by numbers on roll in January, so it can vary from year to year. It is for the school and its governors to decide how it is spent.
Additional LA funding	Additional funding may be given for SEN provision, for the support of ethnic minorities and for those for whom English is an additional language. This is usually devolved funding, not a delegated budget, which means that the school is accountable for spending it on provision for these groups of pupils.
Pupil Premium (£600 per pupil in receipt of free school meals from 2012)	Funding received from central government, to be spent on specific purposes, i.e. provision for needy pupils. It must be spent on this purpose.
School Standards Grant and School Standards Grant (Personalisation) (may be subsumed into the DSG)	Cash payment to schools announced in the Chancellor's Budget statement in April each year. Like the delegated budget, this grant is not ring-fenced.
Other central government funding (may be subsumed into the DSG)	Funding to support national initiatives, e.g. EMAG, School Lunch Grant. Although schools may have some choice on how to spend the money, it's still ring-fenced.
Specific grants from other bodies	The income from successful bids to fund specific projects, e.g. literacy and numeracy (The Basic Skills Agency) and homework clubs (The Prince's Trust). Schools are usually required to match the grant from other sources on a 50–50 basis. This is earmarked funding.
Funding for school status	Income from a successful bid, e.g. for specialist school status: performing arts, sport, technology college, Beacon school, etc. This is devolved funding.
Funding from industry and commerce	This is becoming a rarity! Most businesses prefer to offer goods or services for free or at a discount, e.g. Macdonald's vouchers to encourage school attendance. Specialist school status involves sponsorship by commercial organisations. Specific projects may be funded, e.g. pupil mentoring. Income from industry and commerce is almost invariably earmarked funding.

Source	Comments
Funding from other bodies	Some schools are fortunate to have bequests and donations. These are usually intended for a particular purpose, e.g. for school prizes or helping pupils in financial hardship. This is nearly always earmarked funding.
Lettings and facilities	Most schools have some facilities that are useable by outside organisations. Additional costs – cleaning, caretaking and wear and tear – need to be off-set before this income is included in the school's delegated budget.

NB   Because educational funding is constantly changing, it's important to keep up to date!

How funds can be allocated and spent depends on any constraints such as earmarking or ring-fencing, but for the most part schools have responsibility for determining their own priorities and reflecting these in the funding they allocate to each budget heading.

Building your budget

There are two basic approaches to building up the school's annual or three-year budget. These are the historical approach and the baseline approach. Tables 6.2 and 6.3 summarise the pros and cons of the two approaches.

Historical budgeting is an approach to budget planning that assumes that the school's pattern of expenditure will remain much the same in the coming year. Budget headings are given the same proportion of the available budget as they have received in former years.

Table 6.2   *Historical budgeting*

Plus points (advantages)	Minus points (disadvantages)
• Historical patterns of spending provide a starting point that is reasonably reliable. • Apart from unforeseen circumstances, historically based budgets (with some allowance for inflation) are not likely to become dangerously over-spent in a single financial year. • If it ain't broke, then don't fix it!	• Sometimes a school's historical pattern of expenditure can become problematic without any obvious changes in the school's circumstances. For example, a stable and well-established staff becomes increasingly expensive without income rising to meet it. This is known as incremental drift. • If a school's roll falls significantly, then apparently fixed costs such as buildings and grounds maintenance become a proportionately higher outgoing, and so allocations to flexible costs (such as resources for learning) become reduced. • It may be difficult to fund the school's agreed priorities (as stated in the School Improvement Plan) if all budget headings remain allocated on the basis of previous years.

(Continued)

Table 6.2 *(Continued)*

Points of interest
• In practice, most schools do end up with a budget that is very similar to the previous year's, unless there has been a significant change in the school's circumstances, e.g. a rising roll or a reduction in funding. • Comparison with the previous year's expenditure during the course of the financial year is a useful way of monitoring the current budget.

Base budgeting is an approach to budget planning in which the bare minimum of essential expenditure is identified under each budget heading. The remaining funds available are then allocated to budget headings in accordance with the school's priorities as defined in the School Improvement Plan.

Table 6.3 *Base budgeting*

Plus points (advantages)	Minus points (disadvantages)
• This approach forces a school to re-think its priorities and evaluate the way in which they are reflected in the budget plan. • It's particularly useful to a school that is facing a significant cut in funding. • It's also helpful to a school whose circumstances are changing, for example one taking part in an amalgamation, or a change of status such as moving from 11–18 to 11–16. • There is a better chance of truly reflecting the school's current and future priorities (as stated in the School Improvement Plan) in the budget, than a historic approach permits.	• Effective base budgeting takes a lot more time, thought and negotiation than the historical approach. • Since schools tend to be rather conservative institutions, there is likely to be considerable resistance to any significant changes in the allocation of funds. • There is bound to be an element of risk in moving away from the apparent security of an historically based budget. It would be prudent to ensure that there is a substantial contingency to allow for serious miscalculations.

Points of interest
• A newly appointed head teacher may find this approach more acceptable to the governing body than one who is long-serving would do. In the latter case, it would be helpful to prepare a budget in the established way (probably largely historical budgeting) and present two choices to the governing body.

Now let's have a look at a school's budget and see what it tells us.

Table 6.4 *Melchester High School's budget 2011–2012*

Heading	Budget	Percentage of total spend
EXPENDITURE		
Staffing		75.8
Teachers (full-time)	3,086,500	60.4

Heading	Budget	Percentage of total spend
Supply teachers	50,000	1.0
Education support staff	362,000	7.1
Administrative/clerical staff	174,450	3.4
Other staffing costs	200,000	3.9
Supplies and services		16.6
Learning resources	528,000	10.3
Staff development and advice	29,500	0.6
Catering	192,000	3.8
Other supplies and services	100,000	2.0
Premises		7.8
Buildings/grounds improvements	2,000	0.05
Buildings/grounds maintenance	27,000	0.5
Cleaning and caretaking costs	122,300	2.4
Other premises costs (e.g. energy)	245,600	4.8
Special facilities	1,673	0.05
INCOME		
Basic delegated budget	4,590,816	
Additional SEN funding	123,483	
Funding for ethnic minority pupils (EMAG)	264,015	
Standards fund	361,009	
Other grants	12,000	
Income from facilities and services	58,000	
Income from donations/fundraising	2,500	
SUMMARY		
Total income	5,411,823	
Total planned expenditure	5,121,020	
Excess of income over expenditure	290,803	
Balance brought forward from 2010–11	249,208	
Balance to be carried forward to 2012–13	540,011	

Here are some observations that may be helpful in getting to grips with this school's budget statement:

- The budget allocated to full-time teachers has been based on a 'known' figure: the forecast cost of the teachers currently in permanent posts (i.e. in April 2011) if they remain on the staff until March 2012. The figure allows for known increases in salary costs from 1 September, and the rule of twelfths has been applied. Of course, there may be further changes as a result of staff leaving in August or December. This budget allocation assumes that they can be replaced at a similar cost.
- The budget for supply teachers is a round sum based on previous years' costs adjusted for inflation. If the sum allocated is not completely spent, the surplus will be put into resources for learning. This is an example of fixed-sum budgeting to cover an unknown expense.

- Benchmarking the budget against national figures would show that this is a relatively high figure for support staff. This indicates that a significant number of pupils require support for language or special educational needs.
- The school has a very stable administrative and clerical staff, and so it's possible to make a precise allocation to cover their salary costs. Unlike teaching staff, any progression on pay spine for these staff occurs on 1 April, so the rule of twelfths does not apply.
- The school has had major difficulties in recruiting permanent teaching staff, and is heavily reliant on agency teachers and others on short-term contracts. In order to track and fund these teachers' salaries, they are accounted separately and the overall allocation is based on the number of full-time vacancies (4.5) and the average annual cost of a teacher. The remaining £5,000 is to cover the cost of advertising and recruitment.
- The amount spent by this school on resources for learning (10.3 per cent) is unusually large – benchmarking would show that the usual proportion is around 5 per cent of the total budget. This sum reflects the school's major investment in hardware, software and networking for Information and Communications Technology that is a priority in the School Improvement Plan.
- The budget for staff development and advice will reflect the training needs identified in the School Improvement Plan. It will also include that part of the Standards Fund and other additional grants that are earmarked funding to support national and local initiatives such as the National Strategies.
- Again, benchmarking would show that the budget for catering is at the high end of the spectrum. This school has a very large proportion of pupils who are entitled to free school meals (FSM) and many who are unable to get home for a midday meal. The contract that the school has with a commercial provider will end in August 2012, and the governing body is considering the head teacher's proposal to set up an in-house catering service that will give the school more control over nutritional quality. This will have considerable implications for the non-teaching staff in particular.
- 'Other supplies and services' is a catch-all budget heading that reflects the complex nature of the school community. It will probably include office costs (photocopying, postage, stationery, etc.) and telephones.
- The school has a large and ageing set of buildings that are relatively expensive to maintain in good repair. In the School Improvement Plan, a major rebuilding and refurbishment project will be undertaken in the summer of 2013, with the support of a major capital grant from the LA. The school's own contribution will be the £500,000 that is planned carry-over from recent and current budgets. In the meantime, no improvement work is planned, so this budget allocation is minimal.
- 'Other school costs' is another catch-all budget heading. The school would be wise to account for expenditure on various forms of energy (electricity, gas, other fuels and water) separately. Savings through conservation and shopping around for the best provider can release funding for the school's educational work.
- The large sums of devolved funding for pupils with Special Educational Needs and pupils from ethnic minorities indicate that they form a substantial

proportion of the school's population. Support and special provision are high priorities, and any changes in funding arrangements (such as those that have occurred in recent years) can have a major impact on the school's budget.

- Income from lettings of the Sports Hall and all-weather playing surface, and from providing services (such as the use of ICT equipment by adult education students) make a significant contribution to the budget – the equivalent of funding two full-time teachers.
- The school has very little financial support from its own community. This may reflect the low socio-economic status of the locality. On the other hand, the school may have decided that fundraising is not a useful use of time and energy.

This is a good time to examine your own school's budget and consider how it's drawn up.

Monitoring expenditure

As well as setting up the budget at the start of the financial year (April for LA schools and September for academies), the head teacher and governors have the responsibility of monitoring spending during the year. The information will be provided by the LA or the academy's finance officer, but the strategic overview still needs to be there.

In most budgets, it's unlikely that the monthly outgoings will be a simple twelfth of the annual budget. This is because different budget headings have different patterns of expenditure. These are summarised in Table 6.5 below.

Table 6.5 *Patterns of expenditure*

Pattern of expenditure	Budget heading
Single annual payment	Rates
	Supply teachers (if covered by insurance)
Equal monthly outgoings	Support staff (if no changes in September)
	Administrative/clerical/manual staff
	Caretaking and cleaning
	Rentals
Higher from September to March	Teachers
	Repairs and maintenance
Higher from October to February	Energy (heating and lighting)
	Supply teachers
Higher from April to September	Grounds maintenance
	Improvements
	Reprographics
Lower during August	Office costs
	Telephone
	Consumables
Up to 80 per cent spent by September	Books, stationery and apparatus
No predictable pattern	Other staff costs

Reporting progress

Since legal responsibility for the good management of school finance does not rest solely with one person (head teacher or bursar), it's important to report regularly to the governing body (or its finance committee). The Consistent Financial Reporting format used by schools in their dealings with the LA is not particularly user-friendly when it comes to reporting to governors. I recommend a format shown in Table 6.6. Have a look at it and see what it tells you.

Table 6.6 *Loamshire Education dept., St Mary Mead County primary school budget monitoring report, September 2011, month 6*

Budget heading	Budget	This month	Spent to date	% so far	Year end forecast	Forecast variation	Comments
Teachers	467,353	42,220	207,684	44	461,004	−6,349	
Supply teachers	14,160	690	13,282	94	17,422	3,262	Absence covered by insurance
Support staff	41,136	3,532	19,956	49	41,136	0	
Clerical and manual staff	68,076	5,576	34,624	51	68,080	4	
Other staff costs	3,614	240	3,560	99	5,000	1,386	Further advertising anticipated
Total employees	594,339	52,258	279,106	47	592,642	−1,697	Staff costs balance out overall
Premises	25,552	2,246	13,244	52	26,720	1,168	Oil tanks full, at off-peak prices
Resources for learning	28,130	6,956	23,350	83	28,130	0	
Other supplies/ services	6,950	66	2,814	38	6,950	0	
Gross expenditure	654,971	61,526	318,514	49	654,442	−529	
Income	−2,320	−290	−1,234	53	−2,468	−148	
Net expenditure	652,651	61,236	317,280	49	651,974	−677	
Budget unallocated	27,024		27,024		27,024		Saving for new ICT network
Total	679,675		344,304	51	678,998	−677	

- The school has a very small budget compared to most schools. This means that even small deviations from the planned budget are likely to have serious implications.
- The school is half way through the financial year, at the end of month 6.
- Simple mental arithmetic shows that the teachers employed since 1 September are more expensive than before, as more is allowed to cover the remaining six months than has been spent so far. This is a typical pattern of expenditure for teacher costs.
- The budget allocated to supply teachers is nearly spent. What is the head teacher's strategy for dealing with this? In fact, the helpful note explains that it's a one-off payment to a supply insurance scheme to cover the whole year.
- The non-teaching staff, whose pay increases date from the start of the financial year (1 April), is adequately funded.
- The budget for advertising vacancies (indirect employee expenses) has been spent up. Any further vacancies would require virement from another budget heading.
- The budget for premises costs is more than half-spent. This could be a worry, as the most expensive months for heating and lighting (October–February) are yet to come. This is an example of how a pattern of expenditure is significant in budget monitoring. However, in this case, the school keeper has kept a vigilant eye on heating oil prices and has sensibly filled up the school's tanks during the summer, when oil was at its lowest price. Good housekeeping!
- Most of the budget for learning resources has been spent. This is not a cause for concern, because with the new school year starting in September the school will have stocked up on all its non-perishable resources. This is another distinct pattern of expenditure.
- The school's modest anticipated income is coming in as expected. It's expressed as a negative figure as it's subtracted from the school's gross expenditure to provide the net expenditure.
- The budget unallocated is a planned saving for a specific project; it's been agreed by the LA.
- The year-end forecast is based on both known and anticipated expenditure. The variation in the next column highlights the difference between the original budget allocation and the year-end forecast. A negative figure is encouraging as it means that this heading will be underspent. Positive figures need looking at – it may be necessary to make a virement at this stage to bring spending into line with reality!
- This uncomplicated form of reporting back enables all stakeholders to see the big picture. It's always possible to drill down to see a more detailed picture, for example if the curriculum committee wants to see a breakdown of spending on resources for learning in different subjects. But it does save hours of discussion about the cost of the school keeper's new boots …

Securing value for money

At all times, schools have the responsibility of spending funds wisely and well for the benefit of their pupils. At times of financial constraint, it's particularly important to secure good value for money. More than a decade ago, the government of the time issued some guidelines that still hold good today. They became known as the four Cs:

- Compare how the school's performance rates with that of other schools.
- Challenge whether the school's performance is high enough, and why and how a service is being provided.
- Compete to secure economic, efficient and effective services.
- Consult to seek the views of stakeholders about the services provided.
- More details of how best value can be secured are available on the DfE website (www.dfe.gov.uk).

Benchmarking

One way for a school to assure itself that it is spending money in the best way is benchmarking. Benchmarking in simple terms is comparing like with like. It can be a useful check on your school's expenditure if you can find out what other schools in similar situations are spending, for example on supply teachers. If it turns out that your supply budget is much smaller than the average, then you and your governors might ask yourselves whether you are expecting too much of your permanent staff in covering for their absent colleagues. On the other hand, if you are spending an unusually large amount then you might consider how it might be reduced to release funds for much-needed textbooks.

- It's important to have good quality data. Your Local Education Authority may well publish information about spending patterns in the primary, secondary and special schools for which it is responsible. However, the most comprehensive database currently available is maintained by the DfE on its website at www.teachernet.gov.uk/login.aspx
- It's also important to make sure you are comparing like with like. Data available locally may not distinguish between different types of primary or secondary schools, or between different socio-economic areas where the patterns of spending could reasonably be expected to vary. A good principle to work on is that the more general the data, the less likely it is to be helpful in judging your own school's spending patterns.
- As well as comparing whole-school spending with that of other schools, it can be useful to do some internal benchmarking. Two possible approaches are to compare spending per pupil on different subjects in the secondary curriculum and to contrast the annual expenditure on maintaining the school grounds with what you spend on classroom decoration and furniture.

- You can also carry out internal benchmarking over time. Keep a track of your expenditure on services such as electricity or telephones from year to year. Making reasonable adjustments for inflation, are costs rising or falling? What are the possible reasons? Is it time to look for a different supplier or to change some school practices?
- Benchmarking alone will not give you the answers to all questions. For example, you may find that you are spending 5 per cent more on support and administrative staff than the schools down the road. This may be the result of a conscious policy decision to free your teachers from as much non-teaching work as possible – in which case, your pattern of spending truly reflects the school's chosen priorities. If not, you may decide to review the use of non-teaching staff and draw up a medium-term plan for reducing it when the opportunity arises.
- Look out for those specific factors that make your school different from others. For example, if you have experienced a sharp fall in the school roll then you may well find that as a percentage of your total budget the cost of maintaining the building and grounds is higher than average. This is because the price of keeping the school heated and lit in winter stays the same but your income falls with the number of pupils on roll. Over time, this is a problem that can get worse unless you develop a strategy for reducing costs by taking accommodation out of use or by raising income from letting surplus rooms for other purposes – see the case study below.
- Schools in London face higher overall costs, including the payment of allowances to teaching staff. Ofsted recommends that London schools should add 18 per cent to national benchmarking figures before making comparisons!

Case study: Coping with the unexpected

No matter how carefully a school may plan its financial strategy, unexpected changes in funding (usually for the worse!) need to be responded to. This was particularly true at the time of writing (the start of the financial year 2011–12), when changes in government funding left many schools less well off. Consider the following case study and decide what you would have done as a school leader ...

The school

Towers Primary is a large school (820 on roll) serving a mixed catchment area in the centre of the market town of Barchester.

Until now, the school has been adequately funded and has managed to set aside a considerable sum towards the planned replacement of the ageing ICT resources during the summer of 2012. Owing to unforeseen and unavoidable circumstances, the income on which the school

(Continued)

(Continued)

planned its budget for 2011–12 (see overleaf) has been reduced by £100,000 pa (ongoing). As the head teacher and SLT, you have been asked by the governors' finance committee to advise them on a way forward – they have requested two options for their consideration.

Relevant information

The school mission statement is:

> Aim high.
> Be honest.
> Work together.
> Enjoy what we do.
> Look after what we have.

Staffing

The school is currently fully staffed and there is no superfluity. All but two teaching and support staff are on permanent contracts. The two teachers currently on one-year contracts are Mr A, a full-time teacher of French and Ms B, a full-time teacher of music. Between them, their inclusive cost is £64,000 pa. These two teachers effectively free up the other teachers for their PPA time. Pupils look forward to their French and music lessons. Two other staff are on temporary contracts – a part-time reprographics assistant (£16,000 pa) and an assistant caretaker (£14,000 pa). Currently, the head teacher and deputy head teacher have no regular teaching commitments, but they often help out by covering for absent teachers. Because the school has a relatively high proportion of pupils on the SEN register, the budget for TAs and other support staff is high compared to that for other schools.

The budget for caretaking and cleaning is a generous one as the school places a high priority on maintaining a pleasant environment. The school is also generously provided with administrative and clerical staff as the governors and SLT fully support the principle that teachers and TAs should not be spending their time and energy on non-teaching tasks.

Accommodation

The school is comfortably accommodated in modern buildings that are in a good state of repair and decoration. The site includes a block of older classrooms – a remnant of the former school building – which has been taken out of use, although it's still connected to the main services: electricity, gas, sewage and water. In the School Improvement Plan, it has been identified as a possible location for a Children's Centre, although the LA has not committed to its use for this purpose. A local independent play school and nursery company has been interested for some time in leasing the building for themselves. The school's share of the income would be £12,000 pa.

Resources for learning

Although keen to secure good value for money, the governing body and SMT are committed to excellence in provision of resources for learning. They are conscious that the school's ICT previously leading-edge resources are becoming increasingly obsolete, and the School Improvement Plan includes the replacement of these resources during the summer of 2012 at a cost of £400,000. Annual expenditure on learning resources is about 15 per cent higher than the national average per pupil.

Income

The school raises a modest additional income (£15,000 pa after premises costs have been deducted) from letting the school hall and grounds to a free church that uses the facilities from 9.00 a.m. to 6.00 p.m. every Sunday.

Table 6.7 *Summary of planned school budget for 2011–2012*

Heading	Budget
EXPENDITURE	
Staffing	
Teachers (full-time)	1,501,900
Supply teachers	50,000
Education support staff	216,000
Administrative/clerical staff	220,500
Other staffing costs	10,000
Total staffing	1,998,400
Supplies and services	
Learning resources	137,000
Staff development and advice	10,000
Catering	50,000

(Continued)

(Continued)

Heading	Budget
Other supplies and services	150,000
Total supplies and services	347,000
Premises	
Buildings/grounds improvements	2,000
Buildings/grounds maintenance	27,000
Cleaning and caretaking costs	90,000
Other premises costs (e.g. energy)	125,600
Special facilities	1,673
Total premises	246,273
Total expenditure	2,591,673
INCOME	
Basic delegated budget	2,610,000
Additional SEN funding	61,483
Funding for ethnic minority pupils (EMAG)	40,015
Standards fund	150,009
Other grants	12,000
Income from facilities and services	15,000
Income from donations/fundraising	2,500
SUMMARY	
Total income	2,830,221
Excess of income over expenditure	238,548
Balance brought forward from 2010–11	149,208
Balance to be carried forward to 2012–13	387,756

Commentary on the case study

On the face of it, the school can solve the immediate problem by taking the £100,000 from the planned carryover (£238,548) and settling for a more modest replacement of ICT resources in 2012. However, the reduction in the school's income is ongoing, so it would be wiser to look for a reduction in expenditure that is sustainable in future years. One possibility is a reduction in staffing, and the area for flexibility here seems to be with the two temporary teachers, Mr A and Ms B. But would governors be happy to see the children's curriculum reduced in this way? And who would cover the PPA time for the other teachers? The non-teaching senior staff? Could the above-average expenditure on resources for learning be cut without harming the pupils' learning? Can the school find more income from lettings? You'll see that many options will cause the school to go back to the values and vision expressed in the mission statement ...

Conclusion

Whatever your position in a school, whether you run a department, year group, key stage or whole school, or if you are part of the SLT, it is important that you understand your school's budget because it will impinge on the strategic decisions that you make. A good budgetary understanding will enable you to make more achievable decisions. I hope that this chapter has helped you with that understanding.

Questions for further thinking

- Where does the money come from for your school's budget?
- What are the restrictions on how it can be spent?
- How was your school's current budget drawn up?
- Would you have done the same?
- How does the school's budget relate to the School Improvement Plan?
- What kind of carryover (under-spend) is planned? What's it for?
- Who monitors and reports on monthly expenditure?
- What format is used to report expenditure to your governing body?
- Is this reporting format as helpful as it might be?
- What would you gain from benchmarking your budget against those of similar schools?
- How do you as a school try to get best value for money?
- Who makes strategic decisions in your school? Head teacher and leadership team? The governors? Both?
- The case study – what would be your two options for the governing body to consider?
- How has your reading of this chapter influenced your thinking about how you will lead and manage financial planning when you are the head teacher?
- Do please share your thoughts with me (douglas.macildowie@tesco.net).

Resources and useful further reading

Coleman, M. and Anderson, L. (2000) *Managing Finances and Resources in Education*. London: Paul Chapman.

Ofsted/Audit Commission (2001) *Guidance on Best Value Reviews*. London: Ofsted.

O'Sullivan, F., Thody, A. and Wood, E. (2000) *From Bursar to School Business Manager*. Prentice Hall, Englewood Cliffs: NJ.

Poppitt, D. (2001) *The School Fundraiser*. Questions Publishing: Birmingham.

These publications have a good track record, but in a constantly changing environment the best way to keep abreast is through reading your TES and a journal like *School Leadership Today* (www.teachingtimes.com). Also take a look at some useful websites:

For benchmarking, go to: https://sfb.teachernet.gov.uk/login.aspx

For details of school funding, see: www.teachernet.gov.uk/management/schoolfunding/

To find out more about value for money, go to: www.dfe.gov.uk and do an advanced search for 'value for money'. Keep in touch with this website to keep abreast of a constantly changing funding scene.

Managing Data

Jenny Francis

In this chapter, we will consider the following:

- An overview of the purpose and value of data
- School and pupil data
- Numerical assessment data
- Using data for analysis
- Alternative sources of data
- Easing the use of data
- Beyond the National Curriculum phases

An overview of the purpose and value of data

Data in schools can be the most powerful driver for raising achievement, for identifying barriers to learning and for use when evaluating progress. There is enough data in the average school to fill a filing cabinet in every classroom, if not to fill the classroom itself. Yet how well is that data being used, by whom and for what purpose? In this chapter, we try to unravel a little of the mystery which lies around data and to make it more accessible, useful and less of a burden.

To begin with, what do we mean by data? The *Concise Oxford English Dictionary* definition of 'datum' (the singular term) is 'things known or granted, assumptions or premises from which inferences may be drawn' (2011). So this means we have a whole range of information or data which might be relevant to our key purpose, raising achievement of young people in schools and removing barriers to learning.

School and pupil data

Data might be pupil data or school data. The pupil data is not just a collection of test results but, as we will see, it includes a whole range of aspects. Some of this might be relevant all the time while other pieces of data you may feel are not relevant; but they still exist and may be a factor within the education process of that young person.

School data might be information collected from evaluations processes such as lesson observations, book scrutiny or learning walks. It will include information about the teachers themselves as well as information about physical resources, finances, examination entries, and so forth. External data might come from Ofsted inspectors, local authorities or surveys. So let's look a bit more closely at some of this data and how it might be of value to the school and the pupils themselves.

Types of data

What data might we have?

Exercise

What data do you have about the pupils in your school? Write a list.
Now ask yourself: How reliable is this data?
Who collects it?
Where is it stored?
Who uses it and what is it for?
Write a list of any other data in your school which does not refer to the pupils.
When considering the pupil, data falls into two categories:

○ contextual information: any information about the child and family
○ performance information: prior performance, current levels, expectations and targets.

Alongside this is information on attendance, punctuality and all behavioural issues.

Contextual information

This information, referring to the individual pupil themselves, is usually provided by the parent or carer. However, in many instances, the information is either optional or the classification is left to the discretion of the parents, as in the case of ethnicity and home language, with the outcome that not all of this information is totally reliable.

The following table gives an outline of some of the initial data which may be collected. The reader should consider the validity and accuracy of this data and how it might be used to advantage or disadvantage in relation to pupil progress. A full discussion on such issues is beyond the remit of this chapter.

Table 7.1 *Types of data which might be collected and possible issues surrounding this*

Type of data	Notes
Age and term of birth	Age on entry can disadvantage younger pupils. Conversely, expectation, by age and year group, can limit the challenge offered to an able student
Gender	Generally regarded as a factor in learning styles, behaviours or attitudes to learning
Ethnicity	A variety of considerations may arise from ethnicity, not just from genetic origins but also from where the student was born or brought up
English as an additional language	This classification covers the full range from non-literate in any language to fully literate in multiple languages. Pupils will be classified by their competence in English literacy but for many new learners to the subject, progress is fast once this barrier is overcome
Looked after	A group of vulnerable students, frequently with a complex range of needs, particularly in terms of behaviour and attitudes to learning
Socio-economic group	The indicator of deprivation. IDACI indicator (which schools may not have) is based on the postcode and derived from national data collection. The more commonly used indicator is 'Free School Meals' (FSM) but since this is determined by parental choice it is not truly accurate
Special educational needs (SEN) and disabilities	A range of indicators covering behavioural and learning difficulties, mental and physical health. It is categorised internally by the school to the register of need (SEN), school action (SA), or school action plus (SA+), or externally assessed for a 'statement' of educational need, which brings additional funding to the school. The internal categories are at the discretion of the school and this varies widely in usage
Individual specific information	This may refer to temporary or permanent circumstances in a child's life, such as an illness, family bereavement or child protection issue

This data would also be collated into overall percentage figures for the school. The collated information is frequently made available to the school from the local education authority and much of it is also summarised in the RAISEonline document. In addition, the school would collate information on data such as bullying occurrences, racist incidents, temporary and permanent exclusions. It is the complex mix of these factors, combined with those for attainment, that can frequently enlighten a situation of underachievement and provide clues as to how to address this.

Numerical assessment data

Ability indicators: these are wide and varied but fall into three main categories:

- base-level data (level on entry to school)
- current level of outcomes or performance
- expectations and targets.

There are two key terms which are used in this context. Attainment is used to describe the raw outcomes of the students, the grades or levels which they actually gained. Achievement is a term which is related to progress and, in Ofsted terms, it is used to describe a composite picture of progress and outcomes according to specific guidance in their publications.

Base levels

In the UK, in their first months at school, a child will be assessed, usually by observations, against a range of indicators on the early years foundation stage profile (FSP). This can be accessed from the Department of Education website (www.dfe.gov.uk) and enables a teacher to assess a child across six areas of behaviour and learning, with descriptors for levels of performance, graded from 1 to 9.

Table 7.2 *Early years foundation profile*

Stage	School phase	Assessment style: test = T; teacher assessment = TA
EYFS	Birth to 5; reception	TA: across six areas; 13 categories scored from 1 to 9
KS1	Years 1–2 Age 7	TA: literacy, numeracy, science
KS2	Years 3–6 Age 11	T: English including reading, writing (including handwriting) and spelling and maths (including mental arithmetic) TA: English, maths and science
KS3	Years 7–9 Age 14	TA: English, maths and science, history, geography, modern foreign languages, design and technology, Information and Communication Technology (ICT), art and design, music, physical education, citizenship and religious education
KS4	Years 10–11 Age 16	Optional courses of study built around a core of English, maths and science, assessed through a wide range of external examinations. Key assessment tool is GCSE or BTEC
KS5	Years 12–13 Age 18	Generally a two-year course of study leading to A Levels (GCE examinations), with AS Levels as an intermediary exam at the end of one year. A wide range of alternative courses are pursued, including many vocational pathways

Measuring outcomes in the English education system

Most regions in the UK follow a prescribed curriculum and assessment framework, The National Curriculum, which is divided into key stages, each of which is assessed at the end. Key Stage 1 and 3 results for schools are not published nationally while those for Key Stages 2, 4 and 5 are available. The early years foundation stage profile (FSP) is not published and is not intended as a progress measure for later stages but as an indication of readiness to proceed to the Key Stage 1 curriculum.

Students are able to enter for external qualifications, GCSE, A Level and equivalent at any age, although the outcomes will still be reported at the appropriate time for the key stage.

Using data for analysis

A pupil starting the National Curriculum level will be assessed as to their current performance and allocated the appropriate level, starting at level 1 and going through to level 7 (level 8 in mathematics) by the end of Key Stage 3. In order to track progress more precisely, levels are subdivided, for example level 4 having 4a, 4b and 4c with 4a highest. However, the need to complete an analysis of outcomes led to levels being given a point tariff as indicated in Table 7.3.

A corresponding point allocation was assigned to GCSE and higher qualifications in order to complete the tracking structure.

Although there has been debate regarding the value and effectiveness of this process, nevertheless, for the first time, interested parties were able to compare pupils between different classes and schools. Prior to this time, a parent, for example, might be told that their child was 'good' or 'doing OK', but without the standardisation of levels, this judgement was made purely from the experience of the class teacher and often related just to a comparison of their own class. Not until the child received their final results of GCSE or equivalent examinations at age 16 did they, or others, really have any valid judgement of their ability to succeed against external criteria, comparing themselves to other students across the entire country.

Likewise, prior to this system, there was no objective way to judge if a teacher was providing pupils with effective learning.

In-depth analysis of data

With these point tariffs, it became possible to assess a pupil and allocate attainment scores in each subject. Taking core subjects for the key stage, pupils now had an average point score (APS) and averages could be calculated for classes and cohorts within the school. It now became easy to measure progress of students

Table 7.3   *Point scores for Key Stages 1–3*

Level	Points
W	3
1	9
2C	13
2 (2B)	15
2A	17
3	21
4	27
5	33

Letter grades

A = absent
B = below level of the test
N = took the test but failed to register a level
T = at the level but unable to access test
W = working towards level 1

Point scores for GCSE	
Grade awarded	**Points**
A*	58
A	52
B	46
C	40
D	34
E	28
F	22
G	16
U	0

Point scores for A Level qualifications	
Grade awarded	**Points**
A*	300
A	270
B	240
C	210
D	180
E	150
U	0

by their attainments at specific stages in their school careers. Internally, this would usually be at the end of each school year and nationally between key stages.

Expected levels of school performance

Using the point system, expected levels of attainment and progress for each key stage were calculated and published. These are currently level 2 in English and mathematics for Key Stage 1, level 4 for Key Stage 2 and level 5 for Key

Stage 3. At Key Stage 4, a student is expected to gain 5 GCSE grades at A★–C level, including English and mathematics, although there are also a range of courses which offer allowable equivalent qualifications in both Key Stages 4 and 5. In 2010, the government also introduced the English Baccalaureate, which is made up of English, mathematics, history or geography, the sciences and a language. They also regularly review and publish guidelines on the status of a wide range of vocational and alternative qualifications.

There are also national expectations of progress which consist of two levels (12 points) from Key Stages 1 to 2 and three levels between Key Stage 2 and Key Stage 4. Since it is recognised that not all pupils will reach this standard, the government has set 'floor targets' – basic levels of attainment and progress which all schools should meet in order to be classified as performing at a satisfactory level.

Published tables showing expected progress between levels for Key Stages 1 to 2 and from Key Stages 2 to 4 are available, the latter being illustrated below.

Table 7.4 *Key Stages 2–4*

| | | GCSE grade | | | | | | | | | |
		No grade	U	G	F	E	D	C	B	A	A*
KS2 test level	Other level or no prior available										
	B, N										
	2										
	3										
	4										
	5										

Key   Making expected progress
           Expected progress not made
           Not included in calculation

Target setting

Targets are calculated for individual students using the progress lines for expected progress. The school may increase this level to include aspirational targets and minimum targets or adjust it due to known circumstances about the pupil.

Value added

Pupils are tracked for progress between the stages and a term called value added is used to compare progress to expectations. In its most basic form, this compares the progress of a child to the 12 points expected, while the documentation uses a more complex calculation comparing progress to the average (median) progress made by the previous year's pupils who started at a similar level. Since pupil progress is improving nationally, the expected progress calculated is also rising year on year; hence any school which maintains a steady progress will find itself falling behind the national trend. The difference from expected progress is then centred around 100, that is 100 is added to the final figure (or in the case of Key Stage 4 to 1000) to give the school a value added figure.

However, currently contextual value is no longer used but I will examine it as it is part of your school's historical data.

Contextual value added

Contextual value added (CVA) is calculated in a similar manner to value added but compares the individual's progress to that of pupils with similar characteristics to their own. The intention is to allow for factors which might adversely affect the achievement outcomes of the young people, such as deprivation, and thus place a 'reasonable' expectation on schools and individuals which allows for these factors. However, there is a growing trend to move away from the CVA factor as it can be (wrongly) used to set targets which are not aspirational for particular cohorts of pupils, and thus create low expectations among both teachers and pupils.

Average CVA scores for a school, a specific cohort or individuals can be calculated and, although the calculation is very complex, schools can access an online ready reckoner for individual pupils and are provided with a wide range of ready calculated information for their use.

The RAISEonline document

RAISEonline is produced annually, in autumn, for each maintained school and provides a comprehensive analysis of the cohorts who have completed a key stage that educational year. Outcomes are analysed according to a wide range of criteria and characteristics and provide a printable report or access to online interrogation of the data. In addition, RAISEonline includes target-setting information for the school. However, it does not include any information beyond Key Stage 4. This information is currently available to schools in a document called The Panda. Although this does give information on progress, other measures are being devised, including 'New Measures of Success (NMoS)', a new system being devised by The Learning and Skills Council (LSC). Many school and local authorities across the country currently use ALPs, an independent company which provides extensive reports on outcomes and progress.

Confidence limits and significant outcomes

A reader of the RAISEonline document will notice some outcomes shaded in green and others in blue with the terms SIG+ and SIG−. A green box illustrates that this is a secure and positive outcome, even allowing for the fact that if any group of pupils take the same test on a different day they may perform differently. Likewise, a blue box illustrates that irrespective of deviation on any given day, this is still a significantly low result.

Alternative sources of data

The are many other sources of data, setting expectations of how a pupil might be expected to achieve as well as providing analysis of current cohorts. There are two main providers in usage. The Fischer Family Trust (FFT) provides a range of predictive as well as analytical data. Although the measures of calculation for indicators such as contextual value added vary for that used in RAISEonline, nevertheless the FFT does give individual student predictions for key stage outcomes and for all main subjects at GCSE, with percentage likelihoods of achieving specific grades and levels, as well as compiling expected school targets at differing levels of challenge.

The Centre for Evaluation and Monitoring (CEM) based at Durham University offers a range of baseline tests including PIPs, MidYIS, YELLIS and ALIS, each of which produce a wide range of performance indicators and attitudinal measures.

In addition to these packages, many schools are able to use their own software or commercial packages to analyse data. This may be through a simple spreadsheet or complex structures within the school management system.

The big question in all of this is 'Why do we want to use data?' Is it just a way of adding to performance management? Is there any justification for spending so much time on the analysis of data?

One answer to this has to be: 'If you are spending so much time doing analysis of data that you don't have time to make use of what you find – then don't do it.' (Head teacher in London)

But also, 'Data analysis, if used well, can make an enormous difference to the achievement of the young people in your school; it can make a difference to life chances and self esteem.' (School Improvement Partner)

The reader is invited here to consider the following questions before reading the next section:

What can I learn from an analysis of last year's data which will inform the current cohort?
How can I use tracking data to raise achievement?
What else can data analysis do to help the students achieve?

We need as teachers and leaders to be asking the questions:

How well is (are): my school; my subject/year group; my class; the individuals in each class doing?
And, more specifically, is there a similar characteristic in the group who are underachieving? Are there needs or learning styles being overlooked?

Analysis of the previous year's data does not just demonstrate the outcomes but can identify strategies which were successful in overcoming barriers to learning for the students.

The following list captures a few of the aspects which some senior and middle leaders attending data courses have identified for the use of data in their schools:

- State the individual progress and attainment of any student.
- Set these against targets.
- Calculate class averages in progress and attainment.
- Pick up trends shown by particular cohorts.
- Get expected results (before they leave) for each of the specific cohorts.
- Identify students with slow progress.
- Identify students at the end of any year or key stage who need to accelerate their progress.
- For those who are underachieving, put in an intervention strategy and then create a sub-table to map their progress with this intervention every two weeks.
- Filter the data according to student criteria.
- Filter the data according to any subject-related criteria.
- Have data which is accessible to everyone who needs it.
- Compare rates of progress to national trends.
- Break the data down into subject strands.

Data analysis can only raise questions, it cannot provide the answers and often further evidence is needed to clarify the picture before actions and interventions can be started.

To quote Alvin Toffler: 'You can use all the quantitative data you can get, but you still have to distrust it and use your own intelligence and judgement' (1970).

Here is a typical example of how data might be used: in school X, the vast majority of a cohort was performing poorly in terms of progress in a particular subject. So what was the cause – poor quality teaching and learning, the wrong course for the pupils or something completely different? – and, more importantly, what could be done? What actions should the school take to collect further evidence of the situation in order to make a sound judgement?

The new deputy determined to collect a wide range of data to solve the issue. First, she analysed the data more rigorously. Exactly who was underachieving, and was this a recent thing or had it been a gradual decline of performance over a longer period? Was it everyone in the class, a random selection, or did those who were underachieving have a common attribute such as gender, ability level, ethnicity or a combination of these factors, such as low-ability girls on FSM?

She gathered further data by undertaking a series of learning walks and both formal and informal lesson observations. She watched and listened on the corridors, she spoke to pupils and scrutinised their work. She reviewed lesson plans, schemes of work and resources. She looked at seating plans, time-table issues, gender balance and teaching styles.

Finally, she was able to identify a few indicators which might be crucial. The greatest underachievement was most evident in the most able girls and the low-ability boys who had language difficulties. This latter group were then causing some disruption which prevented others from learning. She was able to offer support to the class teacher in lesson planning, providing pace and challenge to these girls, differentiating the material suitably so that the most able could progress. She was also able to provide a teaching assistant to help with setting the language used to a suitable level to enable the boys to access the materials. Lessons were re-written to include more activities and practical styles of learning, thus engaging more learners.

The outcomes were that learning improved and achievements rose. By using data effectively, the deputy was able to identify the key issues and immediately instigate the most appropriate interventions for the class and thus save money and time, as well as quickly enhancing the life opportunities for these young people.

Easing the use of data

Often the class teacher is inundated with data and is not able to even identify clearly which students are underachieving. In this instance, a simple spreadsheet, as illustrated, could be put in place. This then enables the teacher to interrogate more closely the individuals in the class. What is it that has helped some of the students to achieve as planned and is there a barrier for those still underachieving? What can be put in place to support these learners? It might be anything from extra time, to new resources, speaking to parents or one-to-one tuition.

Table 7.5 *A simple spreadsheet*

Name	English KS2	KS2	English KS3	KS3	Progress points	
A	2b	15	4b	27	12	On target
B	2a	17	4a	29	12	On target
C	2a	17	3a	23	6	Underachieving
D	2b	15	3b	21	6	Underachieving
E	2a	17	4b	27	10	Underachieving

A useful exercise for a team to carry out is to try to place each pupil in their group in one of the nine segments of the table, without looking at their data; then go back to the data and check the accuracy of this.

Table 7.6 *Level of progress*

	High	Middle	Low
Low			
Middle			
High			

(vertical axis label: Level of ability)

A year head in a secondary school may be overwhelmed in trying to check the progress of the groups. In Figure 7.1 an example of traffic lights illustrates how students are achieving against their targets in a range of subjects. The three colours – green, yellow and red (here reproduced in greyscale) – indicate above target, at target and below target respectively, allowing easy identification of rows of 'red' to highlight the need for interventions.

Checking the specific cohorts

It is vital that a school check the relative achievement of the differing groups of pupils by their characteristics. Although individual performance will vary, it is known that some groups of children are way behind in achievement comparisons and that great emphasis is being placed on this by government and external bodies to close the gaps for the future, to ensure that entire groups of young people are not deprived of their life chances in the workplace and in further education.

A particular emphasis currently focuses on deprivation, in this case measured by those eligible for FSM. The following data for 2009 (see Table 7.7) shows how this gap is so apparent at the early years stage and continues to be an issue through to the end of Key Stage 4. The school needs to monitor the situation within its own context and seek strategies to close the gap for this significant group of learners.

As a first review, schools may wish to look at RAISEonline to see how the different groups achieved last year. The CVA figures for specific groups are

Sex	English	Maths	Science	History	Geog	Punjabi	Spanish	French	Art	Music	Drama	Dance	PE	ICT	RE
M	L	L		L	L		L		L	L	U		U	L	L
M	L	M	M	L	L					L		L	U	L	L
M	L	L		M	L							U		M	M
M	L		M	M	L							L	M	M	L
M		L	M	M	L					M				M	L
M	U	M	M	L						L					M
F	L	M	L					L	U		M		L		U
M	L	M		M	M			M	L	M			L	M	M
F	L		L	L					L	L	L			L	L
F	L			M				M	L	M	M			M	
F	L		M					L	L	M	L				
M			M	M					L	L	L				
M		L	M				M	M	M				U		U
M	L	U	L	L						L			U		M
M				M	L					M			L		
M		L		M	L			M	M	M	M		U		
M		U	L	M	M					M					
M		M	L	L	M	M			L				M		M
M			L		L				L					L	
M	L	M	L	L	L			L	L	L				L	
M		L			M			L	M	M			U	U	
M	M	L	M		M		M		L						
M	M		M	L					L	M				L	L
F		L	M						L	M			L	L	L

Figure 7.1

Table 7.7 *National gaps in pupil outcomes in 2009 FSM/non-FSM*

	All percentages	FSM percentages	Non-FSM percentages	Gap
EY good level of development	52	34	55	21
KS1 reading	84	71	87	16
KS1 writing	81	66	84	18
KS1 maths	90	80	92	12
KS2 Level 4+ in English and maths	72	54	76	22
KS2 L5+ in English and maths	20	8	23	15
KS4 5+ GCSE incl. English and maths	51	27	55	28

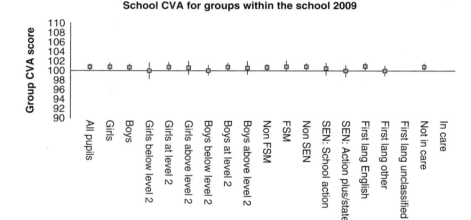

Figure 7.2

available in the document, the illustration here showing the graph of characteristics and a similar one being available for ethnicity. Numerical data is also provided for both of these selections which can be interrogated live to identify the individual's concern.

Other groups for whom expectations are frequently depressed are those for whom English is not their first language. Analysis has shown that, contrary to many expectations, these students generally attain higher standards than their English-speaking peers.

Across a school, the leader would also want to use data in monitoring. As well as looking at an individual teacher to see how the students are making progress against targets, this may include aspects such as:

- Are all teachers making the same rates of progress with their classes (allowing for different abilities and subjects)?
- Do equivalent classes make the same levels of progress year on year?

- Are students making the same progress across different subjects consistently?
- Are late entrants to school provided with suitable targets and do they achieve these?

Combining outcomes with monitoring exercises, it may transpire that a particular teacher is making outstanding progress with, for example, low-ability boys, and this excellence can be captured and shared across the rest of the team. Likewise, where an individual teacher consistently produces low rates of progress for a particular cohort, this can be identified and addressed.

Beyond the National Curriculum phases

This chapter has focused predominantly on Key Stages 1 to 4 but many of the ideas and principles can be replicated in other situations, in private and overseas centres. The necessity is to criteria-reference the materials to be taught, setting them in a levelled approach and determining key time indicators for optimum attainment to achieve the final outcomes. Using tracked data from the most able gives an excellent aspirational benchmark for others to follow. Once this process is complete, it is possible to map intermediate progress along the learning pathway.

In sixth-form settings, the outcomes are measured externally against final attainment levels and many schools use internal systems of assessment to track progress to final grades. The ALPs document is available to those who opt in and will provide a full and detailed analysis of value added and raw performance indicators.

Conclusion

Understanding and analysing data provides school leaders with a powerful tool for determining the effectiveness of learning and teaching within a school. However, analysis alone does not produce good teaching or good outcomes – it is absolutely essential that the information gained is used by the school to address issues for school improvement and professional development, and to focus attention on areas of need, while also allowing for celebration, praise and reward.

Resources and useful further reading

www.direct.gov.uk/en/Parents/Schoolslearninganddevelopment/ExamsTestsAndTheCurriculum/
    DG_4016665
Earl L and Katz S (2006) *Leading Schools in a Data-Rich World*. Thousand Oaks, CA: Corwin
    Press – provides the most comprehensive and straightforward guide on data usage.

www.education.gov.uk – keeps you up to date with the latest government thinking.
www.raiseonline.org.uk – explains the kind of data your school will receive.

References and further reading

Consise Oxford English Dictionary, 12th edition (2011). Oxford: Oxford University Press.

Earl, L. and Katz, S. (2006) *Leading Schools in a Data-Rich World*. Thousand Oaks, CA: Corwin Press.

Kelly, A. and Downey, C. (2011) *Using Effectiveness Data for School Improvement*. Abingdon: Routledge.

Pringle, M. and Cobb, T. (1999) *Making Pupil Data Powerful*. Stafford: Network Educational Press.

Toffler, A. (1970) *Future Shock*. Pan Books: London.

8

Leading the Curriculum

Tom Cragg

In this chapter, we will consider the following:

- Chelsea Academy: Creating a curriculum for the 21st century
- Key Stage 3
- Key Stage 4

In this chapter, we look at the issues involved in decision making around curriculum development, and look at how to get people on board with new ideas and how to involve parents and other stakeholders.

Chelsea Academy: Creating a curriculum for the 21st century

Chelsea Academy is a mixed Church of England Academy for students aged between 11 and 18 years. The Academy opened in September 2009, has places for 162 students per year group and will grow each year until 2014. Planned over 16 years and sponsored by the Royal Borough of Kensington and Chelsea and the London Diocesan Board for Schools, this flagship project has provided school places in an area of London where they were in significantly short supply, and caters for students from a highly diverse range of backgrounds with educational needs across the spectrum. Our aims can be summed up in the Academy's vision statement:

Chelsea Academy aims to create an inspirational community of learning and achievement with high expectations and high aspirations, underpinned by a culture of 'no excuses'. Guided by Christian values and supported by the principle of co-construction, the Academy seeks to bring out the best in everyone, as we strive for excellence in all that we do. No student will be left behind as they are provided with the skills required for life and work in the 21st century. When students complete their Academy lives, they will have the qualifications, leadership qualities and sense of destiny to make a positive contribution to society.

These are the principles on which we have based our curriculum.

Key Stage 3

Key questions to consider when planning a completely new Key Stage 3 curriculum:

- Should the key stage take place over two years or three?
- Should the curriculum be taught through discreet subjects or themed projects?

Thematic vs. academic curriculum

Initially, we planned to introduce a theme-based curriculum focused not simply on students' acquisition of subject knowledge, but also on developing competencies for use and application within the context of their wider learning. This holistic approach to learning, pioneered by models such as RSA's Opening Minds and Learning to Learn, seemed to tie in with our vision for the Academy. There was also a strong case to suggest that designing the curriculum in this way would make the transition process from primary to secondary easier for our Key Stage 3 students. Similarly to primary schools, classes would have been taught a range of subjects by the same teacher and been based in the same area of the Academy for many lessons.

The more we investigated this thematic approach, however, the more inclined we felt to opt for a more traditional curriculum model, where students are taught through a range of discreet subjects. While planning the initial Year 7 curriculum for the Academy, we visited a number of other schools where we witnessed teachers teaching beyond their specialist subject, making us question whether they were playing to their strengths.

Certain aspects of the Opening Minds curriculum and Learning to Learn did appeal to us, especially the concept of students making connections and applying knowledge across different curriculum areas, so although we opted to take the more traditional approach of teaching through discrete subjects, these ideas were incorporated into the Key Stage 3 curriculum in the following ways.

Half-termly themes

Throughout Year 7, there is a specific theme attached to each half term, on which all curriculum areas base their content. The themes are as follows:

Ourselves
Our Academy
Our Community
Our World
Our Faith
Our Futures

In Year 8, the same themes apply, but the level of content is deeper.

As a result of introducing the half-termly themes, it is rare to see a textbook being used during lessons, as it is the theme that is driving lesson content rather than an off-the-shelf, one-size-fits-all Key Stage 3 course from a publisher. With more freedom to focus on genuinely interesting content as well as accelerated progression through the National Curriculum levels, student progress has been either good or outstanding across all subject areas. Personally, in my capacity as a teacher of Key Stage 3 classes, I have felt that by not being bound to a ready-made course, but following a general theme instead, the shackles have been removed and my teaching has moved to the next level.

Personal learning and thinking skills (PLTS)

Having decided to deliver the Key Stage 3 curriculum through discrete subject teaching, we still wanted to incorporate the key skills that students need to embed across their learning, so the PLTS were written into curriculum plans. Every lesson has not only a content-related objective, but also a competency-related objective. Here is an example from a French lesson:

Learning objective: to be able to hold a short conversation about yourself in French
Competency objective: to identify strengths and areas to improve in my pronunciation

As is now standard practice in most secondary schools, all curriculum plans include three levels of differentiation based on the 'all must', 'most should', 'some could' model, but we have also added an extra dimension to the plans, as both subject content and the PLTS are differentiated in this way. The following example ties in with objectives from the lesson objectives above and relates to the skill 'reflective learners':

All must have a general awareness about the accuracy of their pronunciation.
Most should be able to identify specific common errors in their pronunciation.
Some could identify strengths and areas for improvement in peers' pronunciation.

It is a straightforward task to report back to students on their progress in terms of National Curriculum levels, but reporting on progress in the PLTS is not as simple. To overcome this challenge, a set of levels for the PLTS has been developed for students to track their progress in this area, which they fill in on a regular basis during coaching time at the beginning and end of each day. When students have gathered evidence in all of the categories for a particular level, they may receive a certificate during achievement assembly in recognition of their progress with skills as well as their academic progress. This strategy has raised the profile of the PLTS and made students aware that there is more to learning than simply scoring high marks on tests.

Cross-curricular projects

In addition to the PLTS, a range of cross–curricular projects in Key Stage 3 have further encouraged students to make connections and apply knowledge across different subject areas:

- Science and music have created a unit of work on the planets.
- History, art and dance have combined to put on a show about the Wild West.
- Spanish and PE have worked together alongside Chelsea Football Club to teach football skills in Spanish.

Immersion days

Once every half term, the timetable is collapsed and one of the six faculties is handed the entire student body for the day. The rationale behind these days is for students to enjoy different ways of learning and the days also give faculties the opportunity to offer students a deeper learning experience, as they can focus on one topic for the whole day. In a recent technology immersion day (the technology faculty consists of design technology, ICT and business), the Academy became 'Chelsea Pizza Factory' and students attended the following sessions:

- making a 7-inch pizza base and using raising agents
- working in teams to make pizza toppings in a mini-production line
- creating a professional standard food label
- developing a marketing strategy for the product.

To sum up the general enthusiasm for the day, one of the Year 8 students approached me in the corridor, proudly lifted the lid of her pizza box, showed me the pizza and said 'I'm going to take this home for my mum'. The dough was in a heart shape and looked very professional!

In another recent immersion day, the mathematics and science faculty chose the theme of communication, offering students a deep learning experience through sessions on:

- cryptography
- Morse code machines
- sending messages
- animal communication.

There was also a talk based on communication in mathematics from a visiting mathematician.

On this particular occasion, we were told in the opening assembly that we were now attending 'Chelsea University' and students were given booklets that they had to complete in order to 'graduate' at the end of the day. This was an excellent way to raise aspirations in terms of higher education and altogether a very different way of learning.

As well as the obvious benefits for students arising from immersion days, setting up and organising the days has also led to opportunities for staff to develop their skills, for example:

- Teachers have the opportunity to teach out of their curriculum area and in different situations (for instance, teachers who are used to delivering lessons in a classroom experience the challenges of teaching in a practical space and vice versa).
- The necessity to change the structure of the day to accommodate plans has developed middle leaders' timetabling and organisational skills.
- Subject specialists have delivered training for non-specialists prior to immersion days. In some instances, NQTs have even trained members of the leadership team to teach in their curriculum areas.
- Immersion days have become quite competitive, with one faculty trying to outdo the others with their plans. This healthy competition has only served to improve the quality of the events for the students.

Enrichment

Every Friday afternoon, a time of the week when one might expect a higher than average number of behavioural issues to be tackled, there is no National Curriculum in sight, as the afternoon session is set aside for enrichment. Students are taught in vertical groups and staff offer electives in subjects or disciplines for which they have a particular passion. We believe strongly that education goes far beyond classroom lessons, and these enrichment activities do precisely what they say; they help give students a fuller and more rounded educational experience, which builds character as well as knowledge. Known as 'enrichment electives', during the Academy's first year of opening these included:

- Greek studies
- chess
- kayaking
- Chelsea Academy newspaper production
- Future Teachers
- computer game design
- Bollywood dancing
- ancient history and archaeology
- gardening and cookery
- Musicians of the Future
- photography
- cycling proficiency
- dress making with Kensington Palace.

Students' perception of enrichment is 'learning for fun', so when the student council was asked if enrichment should continue into Key Stage 4, the response was a resounding 'yes'. Enrichment has also played an important role in strengthening the staff community, with associate staff running electives alongside teaching staff, and teaching staff from different faculties working on electives together.

The co-construction of learning

At the Academy, we are committed to involving students in the leadership and development of their school. Students, teachers and associate staff are recognised as equal partners in learning, an idea which we have developed in a number of ways:

- Faculties have recruited 'student ambassadors' to assist with open evenings, immersion days, the promotion of the faculty across the Academy, and even the co-construction of curriculum plans and lessons. To give students a realistic experience of an interview process, they are required to write a formal job application and undergo interviews for the positions.
- Student surveys are a regular feature in Key Stage 3, with students' views sought on a range of learning issues. Here is an example of a student survey from the music curriculum area:

  o How likely are you to take music at GCSE level?
  o How much do you enjoy learning music?
  o How much do you like doing the following activities?
  o How difficult do you find the work during music lessons?
  o How do you find the pace of the lessons?
  o On average, how much time per week do you spend on music Independent Learning (homework)?
  o How could your music lessons be improved?
  o Which type of Independent Learning do you prefer?

- Students have played a part in delivering lessons in certain faculties as demonstrated by this list of activities taken from a recent co-construction audit:
    - being given their own roles and responsibilities in group tasks during PE
    - delivering starters in drama
    - teaching whole English lessons
    - teaching a lesson in Arabic on languages immersion day
    - conducting speaking tests (instead of the Foreign Language Assistant) in French
    - taking part in the Future Teachers enrichment
    - teaching maths lessons to local primary school pupils.

Challenges

Setting up any new curriculum model will never be without its challenges, and our Key Stage 3 was no exception.

One of the greatest barriers to teachers achieving what they want to achieve is, of course, time, and starting anything from scratch is a particularly time-consuming enterprise. We have certainly learned that the more bespoke the project, the longer it takes to plan. In order to address this issue:

- regular, manageable curriculum planning deadlines have been placed in the calendar
- wherever possible, faculty planning time has been set aside
- rigorous monitoring of curriculum plans by line managers ensures that the need to re-write curriculum plans the following year is minimised.

As the Academy expands to its full size and the sixth form is added, it will be a challenge to sustain such a strong focus on Key Stage 3. What we have learned, however, is that if you give students an inspiring and relevant curriculum, they can make huge amounts of progress so that they maintain high aspirations and high expectations as they embark upon Key Stage 4.

When trying something new, even if you believe whole-heartedly in what you are doing, it is wise to ask for a second opinion. For this reason, we sought external verification for our Key Stage 3 curriculum. Consultants were brought in to look at a cross-section of curriculum areas' plans, lessons and assessment, including examples of levelled work.

One common issue that will be familiar to teachers around the country is the challenge of trying to keep students motivated until the end of Key Stage 3 in subjects they have not chosen to continue in Key Stage 4. The vast majority of students have remained positive about every subject. Perhaps the most significant reason for this is that they made their option choices in Year 8, but a contributing factor will also be that every student is to receive a certificate for each subject indicating their final level. We have stressed to the students that this will be added to their progress files, so there is still a motivating factor for them. Exams in every subject towards the end of Year 8 are also helping to maintain students' focus on achievement until the end of the year, creating a real 'graduating from a key stage feel'.

Key Stage 4

Key questions to consider when planning a completely new Key Stage 4 curriculum:

- What is the profile of the students based on what you have learned about them in Key Stage 3?
- Which different pathways and courses will you offer and how will you present these to students?
- What guidance will students receive in order to make the best-informed decisions?
- Should there be a two- or three-year Key Stage 4 curriculum?

Key Stage 4 curriculum aims at Chelsea Academy

Before any courses were considered, it was vital to develop a clear vision for Key Stage 4 at the Academy. The following aims were the starting point for the Academy's final curriculum model:

Depth: students are as well prepared as they can be over three years to fulfil their potential in the qualifications they are taking. The gap between A Level and GCSE is bridged as part of GCSE courses.

Quality of experience: students' passion for learning flourishes in Key Stage 4 rather than fades. Over three years, curriculum areas have the flexibility to include a variety of learning activities (for example, projects, educational visits or case studies), which focus on more than the next exam or module, yet complement and enhance students' chosen courses and inspire them to find out more about what they are doing independently.

Support and stretch all students: outstanding curriculum planning ensures appropriate differentiation for all learners.

Skills and qualifications for life

These include:

- a continued focus on PLTS in all courses, making learning as relevant as possible to the workplace and potential career paths
- students taking courses that have genuine currency with employers, colleges and universities.

Early exam entry

Given that we are aiming to provide the greatest depth possible in the students' courses, we decided that our general policy would not be to opt for early exam entry, unless in exceptional circumstances (notably in mathematics where many students may be ready to complete the GCSE course by the end of Year 10 and achieve a further qualification in statistics or even GCSE further mathematics by the end of Year 11). Rather than focus solely on our A★–C percentage, we aim to maximise students' grades in every subject.

An increasingly popular Key Stage 4 curriculum model involves students taking one-year options, which they study intensively over that period. Some schools and academies have found this model to produce excellent results, which they attribute to the immersion which students experience when the recommended learning hours for a course are condensed into one year. After a prolonged period of deliberation, however, we decided that we would not adopt this approach for our students. Many of them had weaker literacy than numeracy on entry to the Academy, and given that literacy has such a profound effect on students' capacity to answer questions across most subject areas, we felt it prudent to give them as much time as possible to refine these skills.

The consultation process

Owing to the vast array of courses now available in Key Stage 4, choosing the right ones can be quite a mind-boggling process, which is why sharing potential curriculum models with colleagues in a range of roles is a valuable part of the process. As ever, using the profile of our students as our starting point, we constructed our curriculum, then subsequently sought the opinions of students, teaching staff, local and national consultants to arrive at the best possible conclusion. A number of publications, including a wide range of case studies into curriculum models, were also used as part of the consultation process, and questions posted on the SSAT's online Vice Principal's Forum led to further views on our offer. It will be vital for this consultation process to continue so that: (a) we remain informed about the latest opportunities for our students; and (b) the ever-changing political landscape is taken into account when considering courses, especially in the instance of vocational pathways.

Pathways

Through their subject choices, students follow one of three possible pathways through the Key Stage 4 curriculum at Chelsea Academy:

- a more traditional, academic pathway consisting solely of GCSE subjects
- core GCSE with a blend of academic and vocational subjects
- English and mathematics GCSE with vocational subjects only.

Art and Design (Fine Art)	Media Studies
BTEC Art and Design	Multimedia Computing
Business Studies	Music
BTEC Business	BTEC Music
Computing	Performing Arts – Dance
Fashion and Textiles	BTEC Performing Arts – Dance
Food Technology	Performing Arts – Drama
French	Physical Education Double Option
Geography	BTEC Sport Single Option
German	Product Design
History	Spanish

Figure 8.1

In order to promote a balanced curriculum, the following subject combinations have not been permitted:

- Business Studies GCSE and BTEC Business
- Media Studies and Multimedia Computing
- Computing and Multimedia Computing

The rationale behind putting all of these subjects into one single option block was an attempt not to stigmatise certain course choices. If we had built explicit pathways into the options blocks, then directed students into the courses, some subjects may have been considered elitist while others may have been seen as 'options for less able students'. In this way, based on their choices and the appropriate information, advice and guidance (see below), we believe students have chosen the right courses for the right reasons. The best-fit version of the students' choices was then created using a piece of software specifically designed for that purpose.

Timetable allocation

Hours per week per subject are allocated as follows in our three-year Key Stage 4:

Table 8.1 *Key Stage 4 allocation*

Core	Hours	Options*	Hours
English	5	Single options	2
Maths	5		
Science	6		
PD	1	Double options	4
PE	2		
RE	1		
Enrichment	1.5		
Total hours			29.5

*Students choose four single options, or two singles and one double, totalling 8 hours of teaching time.

In the case of timetabling the core subjects, we have tried to maximise the opportunity of as close to 100 per cent of our students as possible achieving a C grade or above in GCSE mathematics and English, while science is our specialism, and therefore receives six hours per week. These decisions, along with the timetabling of the other core subjects, were fairly clear-cut and met with little or no resistance.

One of the areas, however, that did cause the most intense debate in arriving at the final allocation of hours per subject, unsurprisingly, was the number of teaching hours for option subjects. Some staff were happy to teach their subject for two hours per week over three years, but others put forward a strong case for three hours per week over the three years. Eventually, we managed to convince colleagues to run with the model above, and our approach to the debate ensured that our middle leaders did not feel in any way begrudging about the final decision, as they saw that it was made with the students' best interests at heart.

Keys to success in the debate (key words highlighted in bold font):

- There were a number of opportunities for colleagues to openly **discuss** timetabling proposals, for example at Key Stage 4 working group and middle leader meetings.
- When decisions were reached, they were **shared** with all relevant stakeholders before they were finalised.
- We were **honest** with staff from start to finish and always made sure that promises were not made that could not be kept.
- During the process, it became apparent that we had successfully created a **climate** where staff felt able to express themselves. When colleagues felt particularly passionate about issues relating to this topic, they felt they could express their views openly with the leadership team. Working in a school or an academy, issues are bound to arise on occasions, but in the climate described, issues are far more likely to be resolved quickly.
- Clear **rationale** for doing things, which was shared with colleagues, meant that they could see why certain proposals were being made.
- Wherever rationale was given for a particular course of action, it was backed up with evidence taken from academy data.
- Staff were made to see how the proposal would **benefit** them. Ultimately, from the data that we generated, the argument that with two hours per week rather than three, staff would have many more students to teach, was quite compelling.
- Running a Key Stage 4 working group was useful for a number of reasons, not least because it gave staff an opportunity to feed ideas into the curriculum design process, and where people see their own ideas being used in a system, they **buy in** to it.
- At the conclusion of the debate, a **compromise** was reached. It was agreed that we would review the timetabling allocation and if it was deemed to be

unsuccessful, make appropriate changes. In this way, nobody felt that they had 'lost' the debate.

- The following quote from the Academy's successful Investors in People Gold assessment shows how colleagues felt about the process:

The consultation process implemented to agree Chelsea Academy's approach to deciding the length of time and number of subjects Year 9s would be studying was effective in engaging all employees, particularly teachers, in the decision-making process. The inevitable conflict between wanting as much time as possible on their subject and the desire to have as many students as possible studying, was thoroughly explored. Interviewees understood the challenges incumbent in the issue, felt that their opinion was actively sought and understood the reasons for the final decision. (internal report)

Information, advice and guidance

One of the most serious questions that was raised as we tried to decide whether or not to run a two- or three-year Key Stage 4 was: 'Will the students have the maturity to make the right subject choices?' Eventually, we decided that the answer was: 'Yes, if we give them the maturity that they need to make the right choices', so developing an outstanding IAG offer was of paramount importance.

Four of the most common mistakes that students can make when choosing their options are:

- choosing subjects because they like the teacher who has taught them at Key Stage 3
- choosing subjects that they think will be easy
- choosing subjects that don't really interest them, only because their parents/carers tell them to
- choosing subjects because their friends have chosen them.

So having identified these mistakes, it was up to us to ensure that they did not happen. Below is a simple timeline of how Year 8 students are prepared to make the right decisions for their Key Stage 4 courses.

Christmas and spring term

All students are invited to take part in the Key Stage 4 student discussion group, in order to share their views and gain a deeper understanding of the options process and courses on offer.

October

In 'My Aspirations' student survey and online forum, students answer questions about their future plans and have the opportunity to contribute to an online discussion with their peers. This raises awareness of the options process among Year 8 students and starts off a dialogue between them about what they may want to study.

December

In an options dry-run, students have the opportunity to fill in a practice options sheet. This provides the Key Stage 4 curriculum leader with important data about potential staffing needs and also helps students to start thinking about their final choices in earnest.

January

All staff are asked to fill in a 'student suitability form' for all students in Year 8. This information can be a useful tool to help students who need to adopt a more realistic approach towards their subject choices, although it is not necessarily a deciding factor.

February

A whole-day 'options conference' is planned to ensure that students are making the right choices for the right reasons. The event includes guest speakers, taster lessons, information sessions and a chance to interview Year 9 students from the Academy, who have recently made their option choices.

February

An options information evening is held to explain the options process and courses on offer to parents/carers. At this evening event, parents/carers and students have the opportunity to speak to teachers of option subjects.

February

All students are interviewed by either their Head of House or a member of the leadership team to discuss both their option choices and future aspirations.

Staff development

A strategy of 'directed staff development' has been adopted for all staff offering courses for the first time. In some instances, NQTs are being sent on courses and then feeding back to their respective teams so that they build a clear picture of what the courses entail by participating in the training, then effectively teach their own teams. This ensures that teachers new to the profession are inducted into Key Stage 4 courses as quickly as possible. On a practical note, it has been recognised that exam boards generally offer their moderation training cost-free up to Christmas, but then private companies charge for a similar training experience after that point, so in order to maximise our resources, staff have been strongly advised to arrange training directly with the exam board during the autumn term.

In an effort to create 'subject experts', staff are generally being encouraged to become subject examiners, as this deepens their understanding of marking criteria in particular.

In CPD evaluations, annual conferences are proving to be the most highly-rated forms of training for learning about curriculum developments in specific subject areas and networking opportunities.

Finally, the other most popular and least expensive form of training has been staff visits to other schools and academies to observe good practice in their Key Stage 4 classes.

Future plans – where to now?

- It is vital that the curriculum remains under constant review, so to this end, student voice and staff voice surveys will be carried out in the near future.
- We plan to create further pathways for targeted students who need alternative provision as they progress from Year 9 to Year 10, and for whom a full three-year Key Stage 4 offer may prove too much.
- We intend to initiate a study skills programme so that students have a range of strategies at their finger tips to revise for exams and controlled assessments.

Questions for further thinking

- What do you think went well in this design of the curriculum?
- What would you have done differently?
- What have you learned from this chapter?

Conclusion

In summary, creating Chelsea Academy's curriculum from scratch has been a rather daunting, yet highly rewarding process. At times, the plethora of courses and curriculum models has been quite mind-boggling, but the students' best interests have remained at the heart of every decision that has been made, which is why I believe that our students have every chance of making outstanding progress over a sustained period.

Resources and useful further reading

Curriculum Briefing is a thrice-yearly journal published by Optimus Education with articles focused on managing the curriculum.

www.curriculum-management-update.com – Curriculum Management Update is a subscription service that keeps you up to date with curriculum matters.

Davis, B. (2011) *Leading the Strategically Focused School: Success and Sustainability*, 2nd edition. London: Sage – brilliant on ideas for building capacity for school improvement.

www.dfe.gov.uk – the Department for Education website with details of curricular changes.

www.itscotland.org.uk – some good ideas on curriculum from over the border.

www.tes.co.uk – some good curricular resources here.

www.teachable.net – quality teaching resources, by teachers.

Leading and Managing Change[1]

Sue Hellman

In this chapter, we will consider the following:

- What do we know about change?
- Models for change
- Identification of the need for change
- Gaining buy-in from colleagues, pupils and stakeholders
- Creating a vision for change
- Developing and delivering sustainable change
- Leadership of change

What do we know about change?

Change is a constant and natural part of school life; however, leading and managing change is a very complex process. Change is not a one-off event that happens, but a process that needs to be carefully managed. Change implies that something will be different, moving from one state to another. In educational organizations, staff will have varying views and emotions about the proposed change, depending on whether or not they perceive there is a need for change and if they believe the change is desirable. The change may be superficial, requiring a slight shift in 'how things are done' or it may be a significant change that requires staff to change their attitudes, beliefs and behaviour.

Activity 1

This activity will help you and your team to reflect on the change process and on what the conditions are for successful change.

Think of a significant change in your professional life. This may be a personal change, a team change or a whole-school change. Discuss in groups your responses to the questions below:

- Why was the change significant?
- What was the reason for making the change?
- What made the change successful?
- What did people do?
- What did people say?
- How did people feel about the change?
- What was the impact of the change on staff, pupils and the organization?
- What common themes can you identify in terms of the conditions for successful change?

Models for change

There is a wealth of research and models about leading and managing change. The purpose of this chapter is to highlight some change models to you, which can be explored further by personal reading, and to consider some key factors in leading and managing successful change.

Thousand and Villa (2001) developed a model for change based on six dimensions. Each of the dimensions must be present for change to be successful. The chart below shows what will happen if any of the dimensions are missing.

Table 9.1 *The dimensions of change*

Vision	Skills	Incentives	Resources	Action plans	= Change
********	Skills	Incentives	Resources	Action plans	= **Confusion**
Vision	********	Incentives	Resources	Action plans	= **Anxiety**
Vision	Skills	************	Resources	Action plans	= **Slow change**
Vision	Skills	Incentives	**************	Action plans	= **Frustration**
Vision	Skills	Incentives	Resources	**************	= **False starts**

In this model, change will only be successful where there is a clear vision for change, where people have the skills and incentives to make the change happen, the appropriate resources and a clear plan for implementing the change.

Kotter (2002) developed an eight-step change model:

Step 1: Increase urgency

Develop a sense of urgency around the need for change. Identify potential opportunities and threats.

Step 2: Build the guiding team

Build a team from a cross-section of people within the organization who will lead the change – the 'change coalition'.

Step 3: Get the vision right

Develop a vision for the future with regard to the values of the organization.

Step 4: Communicate for buy-in

Talk about the vision for change, address concerns and walk the talk.

Step 5: Empower action

Identify and remove barriers to change. Empower people to act.

Step 6: Create short-term wins

Create short-term achievable targets to motivate people.

Step 7: Don't let up

Build on the quick wins and keep up the sense of urgency. Kotter argues that change initiatives fail because success is declared too early.

Step 8: Make change stick

Embed the change into the organization so it becomes part of the culture.

Kotter (2002) suggests that laying the foundations for successful change by developing a sense of urgency, building the 'coalition team' and developing the vision is critical. It is important not to rush the process or expect tangible results too soon. Engaging and enabling the whole organization will build the momentum for implementing and sustaining the change.

Egan (2010) has developed and evolved a three-stage model based on a 'problem management and opportunity development approach to helping'. It focuses on a coaching approach to help people and organizations find their own solutions to problems or 'undeveloped opportunities'. Actions leading to 'valued outcomes' is central to the model. Each stage is broken down into three elements.

Stage 1: Current picture – What's going on?

Getting the story: asking what is currently going on in the organization.
New perspectives: identifying 'blind spots', seeing the story from different viewpoints.
Value: identifying what the organization should focus on to make a difference.

Stage 2: Preferred picture – What do I need or want?

Possibilities: generating a range of options for a possible future.
Change agenda: deciding on a viable option designed to create a better future.
Commitment: generating commitment from people within the organization for the change.

Stage 3: The way forward – How do I get what I need or want?

Possible strategies: generating a range of possible strategies for action.
Best-fit strategy: deciding on the best-fit strategy from the ideas generated.
Plan: devising an action plan for the best way forward.

The above process is not intended to be a linear model. It is a flexible framework to support the change process.

Questions for reflection

- Compare and contrast the models for change. What are the similarities and differences between the models?
- What are the benefits of using a model for change?
- How might you use a model for change in your organization?

Identification of the need for change

There are a range external and internal factors that will influence the need for change in educational organizations. These include changes in national and local government policy; changes in Ofsted inspection arrangement; changes in response to feedback from students, parents and other stakeholders; and, of course, changes in response to the organization's own self-evaluation.

Collins (2001) suggests that it is important to have a deep understanding of the current situation before creating a vision for the future. This involves understanding the 'brutal facts' and 'acting on the implications'. This will involve interrogation and analysis of a wide range of data to develop a comprehensive understanding of the realities of the current situation.

Understanding what is working well within your organizations and why is as important as understanding what is not working well and why. Learning from successes will help to motivate and energise staff, rather than detailed analysis of failure.

Activity 2 (Adapted from TDA/NCSL: School Improvement Planning Framework)

This activity will help you to celebrate what is working well and to identify areas for improvement. It can be used to gain on overview of your educational organization or to review specific aspects of its work, for example teaching and learning, curriculum and attendance.

The activity will work best when you have the views of a range of people, i.e. staff, parents, pupils and other stakeholders.

Once you have decided on the area of focus, ask the group for their views on:

- What's working well and why?
- What's working so-so and why?
- What's not working so well and why?

The questions should be displayed on a large sheet of paper and the group asked to write their views on post-it notes to put onto the sheet.

Once the views have been gathered, they can be grouped into common themes and used to generate further discussion and debate. For example:

- Are the views expressed based on participants' perceptions or based on evidence and, if so, what is the evidence? It may be, for example, that some participants feel that homework is working well, while others state that it is not working well.
- Why is there a difference in participants' perceptions? Is, for example, the homework policy being carried out consistently in all classes? This may need further investigation.

It is important to celebrate the areas that are working well.

Areas identified as working so-so may need minor tweaking to turn them into something working well.

Areas identified as not working may need further investigation to deepen your understanding of the issue.

It is important to prioritize the issues, concerns or 'undeveloped opportunities' (Egan 2010) to work on. There is a real danger of initiative overload as educational organizations attempt to keep doing more and more, in order to respond to these changes. This is not a viable solution for long-term sustainable change. As Fullan states in his book, *Leading in a Culture of Change*, 'the goal is not to innovate the most' (2001: 34). Educational organizations cannot keep doing more and more with the same amount of time, money and human resources without it eventually having a negative impact on the overall effectiveness of the organization.

One strategy that can be used to help prioritize options is to use a prioritization matrix.

Activity 3 (Adapted from TDA/NCSL: School Improvement Planning Framework)

This activity will help you to prioritize activities that will have the greatest impact on the effectiveness of your organization to achieve valued outcomes.

This activity works best with a group of people who represent a cross-section of your organization.

As a group, brainstorm all the potential initiatives/activities that your organization is considering undertaking.

Agree as a group how you will prioritize these, for example potential impact versus ease of implementation (do-ability) and the criteria that you will use to assess this. For example, what criteria will you use to evaluate impact?

Rate each option on a scale of 1–4 in terms of your first chosen criteria, i.e. impact.

Now rate each option on a scale of 1–4 in terms of your second criteria, i.e. do-ability.

Then plot each option on the Prioritization Matrix.

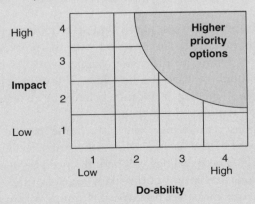

Figure 9.1

(Continued)

> *(Continued)*
>
> The options that have been graded:
>
> - *high on impact and do-ability* will be the quick wins because they are relatively easy to implement and will have a high impact
> - *high on impact but harder to do* will be the longer-term wins.
>
> Other options may need to be abandoned because their impact will be low or they are too difficult to implement.

Collins (2001: 11), in his research on why some companies make the leap 'from good to great', found that 'The good to great companies did not focus principally on what to *do* to become great; they focused equally on what *not* to do and what to *stop* doing'.

> ## Activity 4
>
> Make a list of all the initiatives that have been started or implemented in your organization/department over the last 3–5 years.
>   Now review the list and consider what difference the initiative has made and how you know.
>   If the initiative has been successful, what can you learn from this?
>   If the initiative is not making a difference, what do you need to do differently or can you stop doing it altogether?

Gaining buy-in from colleagues, pupils and stakeholders

Gaining buy-in from colleagues, pupils and stakeholders is essential in any change process. Unless people are on board with the proposed changes, they will be less likely or willing to make the changes work. As Fullan (2001: 34) states: 'It is not enough to have the best ideas.' How people feel about the proposed change, and whether or not they believe the change is desirable, will influence how they respond to the change.

Emotional responses to change will vary. Some people will feel happy, excited and enthused by the change, while others may feel anxious, fearful or scared of the change. These feelings will be influenced by people's experience of change or by their perception of the likely impact of the change on them.

Internal politics can also affect how specific groups within the organization respond to change. The proposed change may have a significant impact on the roles and responsibilities of certain groups within the organization, or indeed their job security. It is important to recognize that leading and managing change is complex and, in order to reach a rational plan for change, it is vital to spend time addressing the emotional and political aspects of change.

Understanding people's openness to change and involving them in the process will increase the likelihood of buy-in and their commitment to making the change happen and sustaining it! Within any team, there are likely to be:

- advocates of change, who are positive about the change, can see the benefits and will make the change happen;
- followers, who do not have strong feelings either for or against the change. They will either go along with the change or will/may have some reservations;
- resisters to change who will point out all the reasons why the change should not happen or would not work. They will try to block the change if they do not believe there is a compelling reason for it.

Activity 5

This activity will help you to reflect on your team and how you can increase team members' involvement and commitment to the proposed change.

This activity is best done individually or with a colleague where there is a high degree of trust.

Reflect on your team and list those people who you perceive to be:

- advocates
- followers
- resisters.

Put a circle around those individuals who have the greatest influence within your team. Which groups do they come from: are they advocates, followers or resisters?

Now consider how you might work with and through those who have the greatest influence to increase team members' commitment and support for the change and to eliminate resistance.

To gain buy-in and reduce resistance to change, Beckhard and Harris (1987) suggested that certain conditions needed to be met. They expressed these in terms of the following formula: **D x V x F > Resistance**

D = dissatisfaction: with the present situation
V = vision of what is possible in the future
F = first steps: achievable first steps towards reaching the vision

They suggest that change will be possible when the level of dissatisfaction with the present situation, combined with a clear vision and plan for achieving the first steps, is greater than the resistance to change.

133

Understanding people's resistance to change by creating an environment where people feel that their voice and concerns are listened to is essential for sustained change. Fullan (2001) suggests redefining resistance as: 'We are more likely to learn something from people who disagree with us than we are from people who agree.' It is tempting to listen to and surround ourselves with like-minded people; however, Fullan suggests that we should respect resisters as they often have ideas that we may have missed or have good reasons for resisting the change. Strategies used to consult staff, parents, pupils and other stakeholders and increase their involvement in the decision-making process will strengthen their commitment to the change.

Case study: Gaining buy-in

School A was experiencing difficulties with managing the behaviour of some students. The head teacher had received complaint letters from some parents. Some teachers and support staff had also expressed concerns. The head teacher decided to form a team comprising of people from across the school who wanted to be involved in finding a solution to the issue. He invited the parents who had written the complaint letters to be part of the group. He felt it would be better to get them on board and involved in the process rather than complaining from the outside! He also involved pupils from the school council, support staff and teaching staff. The head teacher reported that the initial meeting was very difficult as people wanted to offload and talk about what was wrong with the pupils' behaviour. However, the meetings became productive as the group started to look at the facts. Staff were asked to collect data on:

- which pupils were being disruptive;
- what disruptive behaviour they displayed;
- when this was taking place and what sanctions were applied.

By analysing the data on pupils' behaviour, the group were able to get a different perspective on the actual issue. They realized that most of the disruptive behaviour took place during and after the lunch break as unresolved issues at lunchtime spilled into lessons in the afternoon. The group decided to observe the students at lunchtime to find out what was actually happening in the playground and to speak to the lunchtime staff. They also asked the school council for their views on what improvements they would like to see in the playground.

By involving a range of people from across the school in the process, the head teacher felt he now had the support and commitment from people to resolve the issue.

Creating a vision for change

In developing the foundations for sustainable change, I have highlighted the importance of identifying a compelling reason for change and gaining buy-in from those who will be implementing the change. It is also important to develop a shared vision of the preferred future before developing and implementing sustainable solutions. Martin Luther King did not start with a plan, he started with a dream: 'I have a dream.'

Egan (2010) suggests generating a range of possible options for the desired future, before agreeing on the preferred viable option and gaining commitment. When generating possible options for the desired future, it is helpful to be as creative as possible, to think outside the box and focus on the big picture.

- Where do you want the organization to be in three years' time?
- What will it look like?

Activity 6 (Adapted from TDA/NSCL: School Improvement Planning Framework)

This activity will help to generate ideas for a preferred future.

The activity works best with a group of people who represent a cross-section of your organization.

Ask the group to think about what they would like your educational organization to look like in three years' time:

- What will people be thinking?
- What will people be feeling?
- What will people be saying?
- What will people be doing?

Ask people to write their ideas on a flip chart under each section heading:

Thinking?
Feeling?
Saying?
Doing?

An alternative activity for developing a vision for the future is to ask a range of stakeholders to draw a picture of the desired future. Using pictures rather than words taps into the right side of the brain activities and will encourage people to be creative and use their imagination.

Case study: Developing the vision

School B wanted to review and update its vision to reflect the views of the whole-school community. The previous vision was five years old and had been created by the head teacher in consultation with staff and governors. The head teacher was keen to also include the views of students, parents and the wider school community in shaping the vision. The head teacher took various opportunities, e.g. parent evenings and events, school council meetings, governor meetings and staff meeting/inset sessions, to seek the views of each group of stakeholders. Each group was asked to think, from their perspective, about how they would like to see the school in three years' time. For example:

- What will *students* be thinking/feeling/saying/doing?
- What will *parents* be thinking/feeling/saying/doing?
- What will *staff* be thinking/feeling/saying/doing?

Once the views of all the stakeholders had been gathered, a team comprising of a cross-section of stakeholders reviewed and refined the ideas to create a viable vision for the future. In shaping the vision, the team reflected on the following questions:

- How does this align to our values?
- What changes will it require?
- How clear is the vision?
- How do-able is it?
- How committed are people to implementing this vision?
- How will we communicate the vision?

By gaining the views of different stakeholders, the school was able to develop an inclusive vision of the future that all stakeholders could buy in to.

Developing and delivering sustainable change

There are a number of factors that should be considered when developing the plan for change. These will include:

- identifying the gap between the current situation and the desired future;
- identifying any potential barriers to change and how these may be overcome;
- identifying the actions needed to realize the vision and allocating resources – time, money and people;
- creating short-term wins;
- celebrating success;
- maintaining momentum for change;
- embedding the change in the culture of the organization.

If the gap between the current situation and the desired future is narrow, the shift required to move from the existing state to the new state will be small and incremental change will take place. However, if the gap is large, transformational change may be required, involving a substantial shift in people's attitudes, beliefs and behaviour. As discussed earlier, gaining buy-in and commitment for this change is essential. Addressing potential barriers to change at the outset will help to minimize the risk of the change not taking place.

Activity 7 (Adapted from TDA/NCSL: School Improvement Planning Framework)

This activity will help you to identify the potential barriers to change and to identify strategies for overcoming the barriers or minimizing the risks.
   This activity works best with a group of people who represent a cross-section of your organization.

- On a flip chart, brainstorm all the potential barriers that could block the organization achieving the desired change.
- Next, brainstorm all the potential enablers that will support the organization to achieve the desired change.
- Finally, consider how the enablers can be used to help overcome the barriers and record your thoughts in the final column.

Table 9.2 *Barriers and strategies*

Barriers	Enablers	Strategy to overcome the barriers

   Are there any barriers that cannot be overcome and will put the change agenda at risk? If so, you may need to reflect on whether or not the change agenda is feasible or viable.

Creating an implementation plan will help your educational organization to:

- identify the key activities needed to deliver the plan;
- highlight who will be responsible for different aspects of the plan;
- identify and allocate resources, e.g. finance, staffing, training and so forth;
- identify short-term and longer-term goals;
- monitor and evaluate progress against the plan.

It is important to be aware of people's emotional responses to the change as you start the implementation journey. The emotional curve below shows how people may start the process feeling excited and looking forward to change; however, this can turn into frustration and despair as the way forward is muddled and unclear. As Fullan (2001: 31) states:

A culture of change consists of great rapidity and nonlinearity on the one hand and equally great potential for creative breakthrough on the other. The paradox is that transformation would not be possible without accompanying messiness.

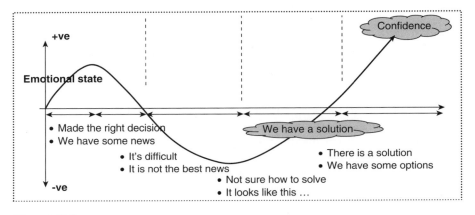

Figure 9.2

Cultural change is a complex and messy process; there are no easy answers and no one-size-fits-all model. Each educational organization is unique in terms of its context, culture and capacity for change. Many change initiatives fail because the journey simply becomes too difficult, so some leaders abort the journey and start another initiative! However, it is precisely at this time that strong leadership is required – leadership that is highly focused on achieving the desired results, that will take the tough decisions and that will do whatever it takes to get there.

Celebrating successes and keeping the plan under constant review will help to maintain momentum and focus. Embedding substantial change takes time, commitment, hard work and, above all, leadership!

Leadership of change

Fullan (2001) suggests that highly effective change leaders are driven by a strong sense of moral purpose to make a real difference to the lives of students. They are focused on improving and sustaining the results and performance of students, not only within their own organization but within educational establishments within their immediate locality and beyond.

Leadership that focuses on people and relationships is essential. Effective change leaders build relationships with a diverse group of people. Collins (2001: 88) suggests that effective leaders 'lead with questions not answers and engage in dialogue and debate not coercion'. They recognize the importance of listening to the views of people who have a different perspective from their own. Resisters to change can bring healthy challenge and new ideas to the debate. However, when emotions run high Fullan (2001) suggests that effective leaders display a high level of emotional intelligence in dealing with people who are resistant to change. They understand that emotional reactions to change are a normal part of the change process.

Effective change leaders create a culture conducive to learning. People are encouraged and supported to learn from each other to improve results. Informal and formal structures exist to support individual and collaborative learning, such as through mentoring and coaching, peer-to-peer support, shadowing colleagues or through professional learning communities and other such networks. People are encouraged to take risks and to learn from their mistakes. If people are not encouraged to take risks, they are unlikely to change their behaviours. Learning is seen as paramount to the ongoing success and development of the organization.

Effective change leaders create the conditions for successful change.

- They avoid initiative overload by prioritizing those initiatives that will have the greatest impact on student learning and achievement.
- They use data intelligently to develop a compelling reason for change and seek to gain buy-in and commitment from those who will be affected by the change.
- They involve a range of people from across the organization to lead the change. This encourages internal commitment to the change as people are involved in the decision-making process rather than being told what to do.
- They communicate effectively throughout the change process so people understand the reasons for change, what the change will look like and how they will get there.
- They understand that transformational change takes time and do not try to rush the process.
- They motivate and inspire people to achieve outstanding results by recognizing and celebrating success. They make it happen!

Conclusion

Leading and managing change is a complex process. Models for change will provide a framework for leading the change; however, it is people that make it happen! Sustainable change will only be possible if those affected by the change 'buy in' to it. Leaders need to create a compelling reason for change and involve people with diverse views from across the organization in leading the change. Developing a shared vision of the desired future and communicating the vision to staff, pupils, parents and other stakeholders is vital. Developing and implementing a plan for change will transform ideas into actions designed to improve student performance and achievement. Strong leadership is required at all stages in the process to maintain focus and direction and to motivate, inspire and empower people to achieve outstanding results.

> ## Questions for further thinking
>
> - How does your educational organization currently identify the need for change?
> - What might you do differently in future to avoid initiative overload?
> - What have you learnt about dealing with people who are resistant to change?
> - What are some of your key challenges in gaining buy-in from colleagues, pupils and stakeholders, and how can you address these?
> - How clearly is your vision understood by staff, pupils, parents and other stakeholders and how do you know?
> - What are the key learning points for you in developing an inclusive vision?
> - What might you do differently next time when developing your vision for change?

Resources and useful further reading

Educational Origami (2010) Managing Complex Change [Online]. Available at: http://edorigami. wikispaces.com/Managing+Complex+Change

Training and Development Agency for Schools (TDA) and National College for School Leaders (NCSL) (2010) *School Improvement Planning Framework* [Online]. Available at: www. tda.gov.uk/local-authority/school-improvement/planning-framework.aspx

References

Beckhard, R. and Harris, R. (1987) *Organizational Transitions: Understanding Complex Change.* Harlow: Pearson, Addison-Wesley Series.

Collins, J. (2001) *From Good to Great.* London: Random House.

Egan, G. (2010) *The Skilled Helper*, 9th edition. Monterey, CA: Brooks/Cole Cengage Learning.

Fullan, M. (2001) *Leading in a Culture of Change.* San Francisco, CA: Jossey-Bass.

Kotter, J. (2002) *Leading Change.* USA: Harvard Business School Press: Boston.

Thousand, J. S. and Villa, R. A. (2001) *Managing Complex Change.*

10

Leading and Managing in an Inclusive Environment

Louise Ishani with Elvira Gregory and Karla Martin

In this chapter, we will consider the following:

- Definitions of inclusion
- Leadership and management in inclusive education
- School case studies
- Understanding context

One of the most challenging tasks for teachers and school leaders is the leadership and management of inclusion. In this chapter, I will draw on some examples of experiences, mainly within the context of British education, examine a range of definitions of inclusion and discuss the complexity of the task faced when trying to lead and manage a school in an inclusive way. In so doing, I will describe elements of good practice as identified by practitioners, commentators and policy makers.

The case studies from several schools are presented to illustrate how leaders and managers in very different settings are reflecting on what inclusion means for them, their beliefs about inclusion and, crucially, how they are using these reflections to create policy and actions that they feel are delivering a more inclusive environment for their pupils, parents, staff and communities.

In conclusion, I will look at the key tasks that school leaders could consider when planning the systematic, whole-school development of good practice towards an inclusive environment for all.

Definitions of inclusion

When discussing leadership and management in an inclusive environment, it is important to first identify what we mean by inclusion. There is, however, no universally accepted definition of inclusion, and many differing interpretations of what is meant by an inclusive environment are offered.

Booth and Ainscow (2000) have helpfully developed a typology of six ways of thinking about inclusion which are worthwhile considering.

Table 10.1 *How do you define inclusion?*

1. Inclusion as a concern with disabled students and others categorised as 'having special educational needs'	Primarily about educating disabled students or those categorised as 'having special educational needs', in mainstream schools
2. Inclusion as a response to disciplinary exclusion	Focused on pupils with 'bad behaviour'
3. Inclusion in relation to all groups seen as being vulnerable to exclusion	Focused on overcoming discrimination and disadvantage in relation to any groups vulnerable to exclusionary pressures
4. Inclusion as developing the school for all	Relating to the development of the common school for all, or comprehensive school, and the construction of approaches to teaching and learning within it
5. Inclusion as 'Education for All'	Created in the 1990s around a set of international policies, mainly coordinated by UNESCO, to do with increasing access to, and participation within, education, across the world
6. Inclusion as a principled approach to education and society	A values-driven approach where the development of inclusion involves practitioners making explicit the values that underlie actions, practices and policies, and their learning how to better relate their actions to inclusive values

For many years, much of the discussion on inclusion centred around educating disabled students or those which the education system deemed to have special educational needs (SEN) and thus requiring something outside the norm in terms of their provision.

This definition of inclusion was limiting in a number of ways: (1) its focus suggested that a child was the issue and did not place sufficient focus on the role played by the environmental context in which learning was taking place as a barrier to learning and achievement; (2) it did not reflect the needs of other pupils who were experiencing obstacles in accessing education or take enough account of social exclusion.

The third definition in Booth and Ainscow's (2000) typology, with its focus on vulnerable groups, takes a much broader view of inclusion and this way of looking at it has underpinned a number of recent government initiatives in the UK, which have targeted specific groups of pupils at risk of underachieving in the school system, for example the National Strategies Black Pupils Achievement Projects in the UK. This shift in viewing inclusion began in the UK with The Warnock Report in 1978, followed by the 1981 Education Act. These led to a real change in the language used to describe inclusion practice in schools, with a much greater focus on a common educational framework, which ultimately led to the introduction of the National Curriculum in 1992 and goals for all children, regardless of their abilities or disabilities, focused on developing independence and enjoyment. Focusing on vulnerable groups highlighted the importance of understanding barriers to learning and participation and the importance of increasing the capacity of all schools to support learning and participation in response to pupil diversity (Booth and Ainscow, 2000).

More recently, the broader term additional educational needs (AEN) has been used by policy makers in the UK to refer both to the needs of pupils with SEN and to the needs which may be experienced by pupils from particular social groups whose circumstances or background are different from most of the school population, such as Gypsy, Roma and Traveller Pupils or pupils with English as an additional language. Additional Support Needs (ASN) is another term which has gained currency and it has a much broader scope. ASN applies to children and young people who, for whatever reason – social, emotional, cognitive, linguistic, disability, or family and care circumstances – experience barriers to their learning and therefore require additional support for a period of time, in order to help them make the most of their school education.

The changing focus in the use of AEN and ASN instead of SEN is under-pinned by a shift in pedagogical thinking described by Florian and Black-Hawkins (2010) as a pedagogy which focuses on how to 'extend what is ordinarily available in the community of the classroom as a way of reducing the need to mark some learners as different … providing rich learning oppor-tunities that are "sufficiently" made available for everyone, so that all learners are able to participate in classroom life'.

The sixth definition in Ainscow's typology describes a values–driven approach to inclusion. In this definition, the development of inclusion involves practitioners first making explicit the values that underlie actions, practices and policies and, second, their learning how to better relate their actions to inclusive values (Ainscow et al., 2006). This definition is based on the belief that values underlie all actions and plans of action, all practices within schools, and all policies for the shaping of practice. This links to Michael Fullan's work on moral purpose (2001) and is based on the belief stated by Ainscow et al. (2006) that we cannot do the right thing in education without understanding at some level the values from which our actions spring.

How you see inclusion will ultimately define what you see as an inclusive environment. Gaining a consensus about what is understood about inclusion in your school context will underpin what you see as contributing to having an inclusive environment in your school.

It is 'natural' for teachers and school leaders to be concerned with inclusion in terms of teaching in the classroom, but what this brief review of definitions hopefully shows is a need to think in a much broader way, which includes a focus on the educational experience of a child in the whole school and in other contexts outside the school, including the home.

Leadership and management in inclusive education

This chapter focuses on case studies from schools that exemplify the broader definitions of inclusion, which encompass pupils with additional education needs, to identify good practice.

A recent study was carried out by the National College in the UK, working with head teachers and school leaders involved in the national strategies pilot programme 'Achievement for All' which focused on improving outcomes for special educational needs and or disability (SEND). This study identified four key characteristics relating to the effective leadership and management of SEND, and we believe these can be applied more broadly to the management of inclusion:

- a shared vision – a core set of values and beliefs, shared by all staff, that all children and young people have the right to opportunities to develop their learning
- commitment – to creating an ethos and culture of achievement across the whole school, a determination to secure the best provision for vulnerable children and young people and to provide effective continuing professional development for staff
- collaboration – with parents, children and young people and others within and beyond the school, including other schools, to develop and share best practice
- communication – with and between children and young people, their parents, staff, other schools and other agencies (Bennett, 2010).

The next part of this chapter will examine how a number of schools have approached the leadership and management of inclusion.

School case studies

John Donne Primary School

At John Donne Primary School in Peckham, London (Southwark LA), the joint head teachers are Evelyn Holdsworth and Nick Tildesley. The school has a values-driven approach to leading and managing in an inclusive environment.

John Donne School is situated in the heart of Peckham, a vibrant, exciting and multi-cultural area in south-east London. I visited this community primary school in spring 2011 and spoke to school leaders about their approach to creating, leading and managing an inclusive environment.

The first thing I wanted to find out is how the head teachers defined inclusion in their context:

We would define an inclusive environment as one where every-body is contributing to the school. By everybody we mean all stakeholders. We see the school as acting as a catalyst within the community. Our view is centred in the belief that people work bet-ter when they are valued and everyone should be given the oppor-tunity to take chances, be brave, try things out and grow. We think this is really important in a context where many parents have had difficult educational experiences themselves. For us inclusion is not just about special educational needs (SEN); we believe every-body has gifts, skills, a culture that they can share, every person has something to contribute to this community and for us being inclusive is about how we enable people to share and access it.

We believe inclusion equals an approach to life, not a list of activities. We like to use the analogy of family when we think about inclusion. Inclusion in our context is what happens when there isn't anything so bad that can happen that you can't be reconciled to the community.

Evelyn Holdsworth and Nick Tildesley, joint head teachers

In talking to the head teachers, it was clear that the most important thing to them in terms of leading inclusion and creating an inclusive

(Continued)

(Continued)

community was being explicit about the core values that underpin the school's ethos and culture. These values were influenced by the context of the school and the community that it was a part of. Values drove the choice of activities and the way in which the school was structured and led.

We asked the school to give us some examples of how this focus on values influenced practice in their school:

1. **Distributed leadership.** The very fact that the school has joint head teachers has helped shape their commitment to distributed leadership. Having joint head teachers naturally facilitates shared leadership and honest conversations about what they really want for the school as a team and what that should look like. The joint head teachers have created a 'flat' leadership structure, leading to a broad strategy team which they say allows free flow of information, challenge and support. They describe how they strove to create a structure which provided school leaders with a significant degree of independence in their leadership, allowing space for people to grow. The school has phase leaders who are given school data and improvement priorities to focus on. They use these to create action research projects where they analyse issues and design projects to tackle key priorities. The school feels it has created a sustainable leadership structure which allows the school to function effectively even when both head teachers are not present.

2. **High aspirations**. Both head teachers at John Donne School were very clear that, for them, it was not enough just to talk about values; being inclusive is about being successful: 'The needier the community you serve the more you need to inspire.'

   Inclusion is also about the achievement of pupils and their families. This year, during a discussion at the school's governing body meeting, a parent governor shared the fact that her daughter wanted to be a doctor and that they had visited lots of universities together. She described how on each occasion she was the only black parent present. When she had mentioned in these meetings that she was a Peckham parent, she sensed the other parents sniggering. There was clearly not the expectation that pupils from Peckham would go on to become doctors. The governors felt they wanted to do something in response and wanted to work with pupils at John Donne and their parents on aspirations. As a result, the school has organised a visit to Cambridge University for Year 6 pupils and their families.

3. **Curriculum planning**. The school has built within the structure for curriculum planning a section for including values. These values inform curriculum content. The school uses the Centre for Literacy in Primary Education (CLPE) Power of Reading programme, which has books which are all 'challenging reads' dealing with major issues and themes. Each class in the school uses one book per her half term as a core stimulus for learning.

Another part of their inclusive curriculum involves the teaching of 'Philosophy for Children' once a week. This begins in Key Stage 1 and engages pupils in focusing on values-related texts, in order to have discussion and help them understand from a very young age the value of everyone having a right to have their opinion heard.

The school considers music and singing to be an important part of its approach to creating an inclusive environment. It has employed music specialists to support singing across the school and to provide professional development for teachers. There is a children's choir where pupils have to audition to become part of it:

Being part of the choir gives pupils status. The school has now given pupils the opportunity to have additional singing lessons along the lines of instrumental lessons which allow the pupil opportunity to sit grade exams. These exams support pupils at the school in applying for music scholarships for secondary school places. (Nick)

4. **Use of physical space**. The school has recently modified its own reception space, providing a more open accessible space for parents and visitors on arrival. The school feels this is important in creating a more welcoming school and is part of its inclusive approach: 'The welcome at a school can demonstrate the ethos/climate of the school. Lack of welcome can be about the physical space, not just the interaction with school staff' (Evelyn).

5. **Engagement with parents and the community**. 'People work better when they are valued. We see the school as a positive catalyst in the community. We spend a lot of time making it explicit to parents that we want the school to do well and they like the fact that we take the time to talk to them and included them in the conversation about school improvement' (Nick).

The head teachers described how it takes time to get to know and understand the community and its needs, and how the school has organised activities to meet those needs in partnership with local organisations.

(Continued)

(Continued)

The school has a weekly parents' coffee meeting and also works with individual parents to help meet their specific needs. They describe how they recently worked with a parent with epilepsy who couldn't write. The school used its links to enrol her on a course which allowed her to obtain a qualification, something that she is really proud of.

We carry out a variety of questionnaires to find out parents' views and each year in the summer term we have two days where we also run workshops for parents in partnership with local organisations. The local credit union, police, local health organisations come and run workshops in the schools. The feedback from parents is that they like what is happening; therefore there is much less pupil mobility, even in an area of high social mobility. (Evelyn)

6. **Valuing community culture**. The school values the richness of the cultures of the local community and uses its carnival, which takes place every other year, as a strategic way of being inclusive of local families' and communities' cultures: 'Food is a universal language – people want to share what they are proud of; they want to showcase something of their culture, food, dress' (Nick).

7. **Staff wellbeing**. I was interested to know how the school knew whether staff felt they were included.

We have a large leadership team divided into phases led by phase leaders. Phase leaders have responsibility for 3–4 teachers and staff. As head teachers we meet regularly with phase leaders to find out how things are going. Do people feel included? This will depend on their definition of inclusion. The school has a staff wellbeing committee. This committee has recently reviewed the staff handbook and this has led to discussion about ways of working. The committee has responsibility for looking at levels of social activity, i.e. they set up activities for staff, e.g. masseurs. The committee is open to all staff to join. (Nick)

8. **Staff development**. 'In an inclusive community we hope to see respectfulness in the relationship and interactions between children and adults – in a broad sense this doesn't always happen all the time; but we see this as part of the continuous learning for staff which is a key part of our inclusive approach. Providing opportunities for staff to reflect away from school is something we think is important' (Evelyn).

9. **Targeted interventions for underperforming groups of pupils**. I asked if their school had any underperforming groups of pupils and whether they worked in a particular way to support the inclusion of these pupils.

Our school data tells us that in the early years the underperforming groups are the White British boys. In KS1 it is Black Caribbean boys. However, by the end of KS2 both groups catch up. We have a learning mentor and parental support advisor who work with small groups on a regular basis to talk through motivation and ways of working and set individual weekly targets for their groups. Progress is reported to the head teachers every week with a sense of achievement as pupils work through their targets. (Nick)

Conclusion

Nick and Evelyn believe that the culture and ethos of their school is key to creating an inclusive leadership environment. They believe it is not enough for leaders to think about sets of actions, they need to first be clear about their values and these, together with their particular context, should drive the actions that leaders choose. They believe the key to success is a commitment to providing the best quality actions to achieve good outcomes for pupils and their families. The key, they believe, is getting enough people to commit to these values.

Hampstead Secondary School

At Hampstead Secondary School, London (Camden LEA), Heather Daulphin is the deputy head teacher. The goal here was improving behaviour and academic performance by focusing on the teaching of active listening strategies.

Background

Hampstead School had identified poor listening as an issue that was frustrating to teachers and affecting the behaviour and academic performance of students in class. They successfully bid to take part in a research-based project. This was the Listen EAR Project, which offered the time of a speech and language therapist to work alongside staff to

(Continued)

(Continued)

develop listening strategies in the school. The project was incorporated into the Achievement for All (AfA) project, a national strategies funded project that was being piloted in the LA. With a focus on Year 7 and Year 8, they hoped the project would help the school to address a number of key aims:

1. To embed a positive culture of listening and communication skills into the daily functioning of the school.
2. To raise the profile of communication and listening skills across the curriculum delivery.
3. To empower teachers in supporting pupils with difficulties in listening and communicating appropriately, including a significant number of pupils with EAL and speech difficulties.
4. To test the theory that improving listening and communication can in turn improve behaviour and academic performance.
5. To encourage consistency of approach and consistent use of specific strategies to support listening.

What was done and how?

The AfA project worker and the Listen EAR project speech and language therapist carried out a baseline audit of listening skills and the strategies used by teachers to support listening. Lesson observations took place and the findings were presented to the SLT and staff as part of a whole-school inset and also to governors.

Following the audit, the school's action plan was devised and SEND staff delivered a programme of staff inset which focused on 'Can't listen – won't listen'. These insets provided training for staff on supporting pupils with difficulties in listening and communicating appropriately and provided a highly structured approach and specific strategies to support listening which could be used with the whole class. Resources were created and shared with staff to support listening skills. These resources included visual support strategies, 'the five rules of listening' posters, PowerPoint presentations on listening for use with pupils, active listening lesson plans, listening starter activities (both topic and non-topic related), and management tools such as learning walk scripts. In addition, all Year 7 and Year 8 classes received two responsible listening lessons which involved the project leads in team teaching with the year group tutors.

Hampstead School uses the 'I-behave' reward system and they decided to incorporate the active listening behaviours into this system so that individuals and groups of pupils could receive rewards for demonstrating good awareness of 'the five rules of listening'. Listening week was introduced as a strategy for raising awareness of listening strategies among students and a way of rewarding the positive learning behaviours linked with active listening. This was held in February 2010 with lessons and competitions linked to listening, and rewards for pupils.

Hampstead trained its support staff to deliver active listening groups for students with SLCN (Speech Language and Communication Needs). The groups ran in the autumn term of 2009 and spring term of 2010 and involved 12 students in total. Each group received two sessions of intensive active listening support per week. The school is now using lesson observations to monitor these pupils' progress in class and to identify a new cohort to attend the group.

At Hampstead, it was felt important to involve parents/carers in the project and all Year 7 parents/carers were sent letters about the project in September 2009, which were followed up with a presentation at the parents/carers' induction meeting and by an invitation to attend a parents' workshop in listening week.

Impact and evidence

The school has set up a detailed monitoring and review programme to measure the impact of the project. Feedback has been collected from students and staff on the impact of the project, and a programme of lesson observations was carried out and supported by the speech and language therapist. The project has already been extremely successful, with pupils and staff commenting on the improved learning outcomes and learning behaviour.

The school saw a significant increase in levels of listening behaviour during the listening week and a marked increase in students' motivation in learning. The number of 'I-behave' rewards quadrupled in one week as pupils were keen to be rewarded for good listening and knew exactly how to gain the rewards because they had been given really clear criteria for doing so.

The feedback from the listening workshop for parents/carers was extremely positive and parents/carers were particularly grateful for the range of handouts provided on communicating with their sons/daughters. The school intends to follow up this workshop with another focused on parents/carers of sons/daughters with SLCN.

(Continued)

(Continued)

Lessons learnt and next steps

The next step is making an explicit link to the school's teaching and learning policy. The school believes it will really begin to see the impact of the project when it becomes part and parcel of the school's behaviour for learning work and when it is clearly linked to teaching rules, the curriculum and the use of rewards and sanctions.

The project is now offering training with a focus for individual teachers, curriculum departments and whole-school year-group delivery. The Maths, Humanities and Drama departments and Year 11 are all currently involved. The school is using the AfA project to support staff using the lesson study model, which allows staff to work in teams of three to develop their own practice and which will help to further embed consistency across the school. Each teacher focuses on three SEND pupils in their class and looks at whether they can improve the learning for those pupils with an improved listening goal.

Acland Burghley School

At Acland Burghley School in London (Camden LA), the focus in this study was the use of structured parent conversations to support a Year 10 pupil with communication difficulties and attendance issues (Jo Armitage, Headteacher).

At Acland Burghley, the use of parent conversations proved very effective in supporting a pupil who had been very withdrawn and who had experienced issues with his self-esteem and in developing relationships with his peers and adults. The school had specifically set aside some of its funding, which it received as part of the Achievement for All (AFA) project, to provide interventions for Year 10 pupils.

What was done and how: the school held a parent conversation meeting with the pupil's parents in November 2009 and March 2010 and these allowed the school to gather a lot of information regarding how he was coping with his coursework and academic work. It was clear from the conversations that his parents had with us, that they had previously been in the dark about his issues with academic work and were not fully aware of his struggles. The conversation provided the forum for this particular pupil to have a discussion with his parents about coursework, highlighting what he wanted in the way of support. The conversations also provided an opportunity for these parents to highlight areas of his coursework that they were concerned about.

Impact and evidence: as a result of these conversations, subject teachers were informed of the concerns raised by both the pupil and his parents. Teachers in turn made contact with the parents of the pupil and provided support and information about the curriculum. This support helped the parents to feel less anxious and made them feel more able to track and support their child's progress more effectively.

Acland Burghley has a number of Year 10 SEND pupils with difficulties with attendance and social and communication skills, which impacts on their capacity to do coursework. One-to-one tutoring delivered by LSAs (Learning Support Assistants) or teachers is offered to these pupils to help them before a problem with coursework spirals out of control. Pupils decide what subject they would like tutoring in, with an input in the decision from tutors, teachers and parents. This particular pupil received a programme of weekly one-to-one tuition in science and maths. He liked rewards and the parent conversations were used to agree school rewards and family rewards for progress which acted as a motivator for him.

The conversations particularly helped this pupil to have important conversations with his parents that he would not have felt able to initiate otherwise. They helped his teachers to realise he was a shy pupil, as opposed to someone who they might have thought was a work avoider and not interested in achieving. They were able to share this information with other staff who worked with him, which gave them greater understanding of how to work with him.

> I want a good start to Year 11. Maths tutoring has really helped. It's what I needed. If I had had it in other years it would have been better. I am doing much better than last year. Last year I couldn't do anything. I was struggling. I am much faster in my work ... I am proud of doing better in class. I did five pages of writing in English rather than one page. (A supported pupil)

Lessons learnt and next steps

For Year 10, the conversation about the pupils' home background is really important as it allows parents to be able to talk about what they see are the issues. It makes them believe the school is interested and creates a partnership which allows the school to push the academic issues to the forefront.

Camden Secondary Learning Support Service

At Camden Secondary Learning Support Service in London (Camden LA), Gabriella Thomas is the Teacher in Charge. This particular case study frames the effective leadership and management of staff within a Key Stage 3 Pupil Referral Unit (KS3 PRU) and shows how it was supported through meeting the staff team's needs, to enable them to meet the needs of the students.

The context is constructed through looking at levels of staff and student need, within Maslow's hierarchy of needs. It specifies the structures, policies, ways of working and behaviours, which underpin the effective leadership and management of the PRU.

Key principals of our approach to leadership and management

- Meeting the needs of students by meeting the needs of staff, so that staff are better able to take up their roles in relation to students.
- Making staff feel secure and confident, so that they can be open, creative, innovative and sensitive.
- Knowing that creating such a safe, holding environment for staff and students is a constant, ongoing process.

Level of need – physiological needs and safety

Table 10.2 *Physiological and safety needs*

Students	Staff team
• Food • Clean environment • Clear boundaries, expectations and consequences • Consistency • Stable, predictable relationships • Excellent teaching • Target-setting • Points system • Tracking • Restorative language	• Health and safety procedures • Policies and procedures • Briefing/debriefing • Risk assessment and management • Rigorous performance management • Training • CPD • Rigorous recruitment, selection and induction • Restorative language

Specific to the PRU

A restorative approach

This is an embedded approach to prevent and manage conflict which embodies the use of restorative language; the use of circle time as a whole provision and in classes; class agreements; class social targets; and restorative meetings/conferences to resolve incidents of conflict.

Daily briefing and debriefing sessions

These are information-sharing sessions which give staff the opportunity to discuss students, raise concerns, and seek advice and guidance from the team. A clear structure, purpose and solution-focused approach keeps the sessions focused and prevents them from simply becoming a time for 'off-loading'.

Points system

The system of points, which are received in every lesson in relation to levels of engagement, behaviour, participation and effort, enables teachers to track student progress, triggering intervention and reward as appropriate.

Level of need – love and sense of belonging

Table 10.3 *Love and a sense of belonging*

Students	Staff team
• Relationships • Activities • Trips • Individualised, personalised, tailored curriculum • Opportunities for 1:1 teaching • Mentoring • Review meetings • Communication and engagement with parents/carers • Community events • Assemblies • Class agreements • Restorative practices • Displays • Reports • Community presence in using local resources	• Transparency about ways of working and rationale • Collaborative working • Individual roles and responsibilities • Individualised training • Regular staff consultation meetings • Daily briefing/debriefing • Training • CPD • Individual support • Shared ownership, vision, commitment, passion, attitude • Restorative practices • Shared humour! • Social events

(Continued)

(Continued)

Specific to the PRU

Staff consultation meetings

Led by clinical psychologist attached to the PRU, they are an opportunity for the whole staff team to think together about particular concerns, dilemmas, successes and experiences. It is a regular open forum that aims to share thinking, develop ongoing assessments and refine interventions with students, as well as providing support for staff.

Level of need – esteem

Table 10.4 *Esteem*

Students	Staff team
• Weekly assemblies, with rewards and recognition • Praise • Successful transition	• New developments • New opportunities • Creativity • Monitoring, feedback and evaluation • Currently – new practice framework

Specific to the PRU

The New Practice Framework

This is a 'live' document that combines the theory and practice underpinning the work in the PRU. The rationale for the unit's ways of working incorporates psychological, neurological and behavioural approaches. These are combined with applicable ideas from attachment theory to generate strategies for interventions and behaviour management for individuals and groups of students. The framework is reviewed and updated termly with the whole staff team and is a key document in supporting staff to understand and meet the needs of the unit's challenging cohort. The framework is for existing staff, new staff and for sharing with colleagues.

Level of need – self-actualisation

Table 10.5 *Self-actualisation*

Students	Staff team
• Fulfilling potential • Returning to mainstream school • Moving to an appropriate educational provision • Remaining engaged in education	• Feedback from students, parents/carers, ex-students, peers and colleagues • Development • Creativity • Moving on • Training others • Delivering workshops and presentations nationally

Paul Greenhalgh (1994), in writing about emotional growth and learning, describes how adults and individuals in schools play a key role in helping children to work through 'anxiety and disturbing feelings'. He talks about 'emotional holding' and this concept is key to the success of the approach adopted by Gabriella Thomas, the teacher in charge at the Camden KS3 PRU. Creating such a safe, holding environment for staff and students is a constant, ongoing process at the PRU. Meeting the needs of staff, so that they are better able to take up their roles in relation to students and feel more secure and confident in being open, creative, innovative and sensitive, is an approach to the leadership of inclusion which we feel would benefit all schools.

Case studies – conclusion

These case studies highlight clearly that inclusion encompasses all aspects of schools. When it is done well, it is at the core of a school's overall values, ethos, culture and, ultimately, academic success and effectiveness.

Understanding context

Context has an impact on what inclusion looks like from school to school, borough to borough and situation to situation. It is essential for school leaders to have the contextual literacy that will enable them to make provision for all that is necessary to meet the needs of all children equally well.

A secure knowledge and understanding of context, whether it is the unique experience and strengths children and families bring to the community or the barriers that they may face or have experienced, is as important as nurturing staff capacity and demonstrating ability to create a vision and an environment that will allow a school community to grow and succeed.

Conclusion

As leaders, you need to clarify what you perceive inclusion to be, understand the way in which it can potentially transform the educational experience of everybody and be prepared to find out and assess the impact of every action on the whole school and all stakeholders.

In *The Need to Belong: Rediscovering Maslow's Hierarchy of Needs* (1992), Kunc states that he believes valuing diversity in the human community is a fundamental principle of inclusive education. He goes on to identify the importance of 'looking beyond typical ways of becoming valued members of the community' if we want to make giving all children an authentic sense of belonging a reality. Central to his thinking is the need for educationalists to move away from the belief that we need to 'normalise' children in order for them to contribute in the typical ways the school system expects. In a number of the case studies contained in this chapter, we see the importance of creating a sense of belonging to successfully and effectively facilitate the work of staff and the achievement of pupils who, in a traditional sense, do not fit the 'norm'.

Questions for further thinking

- What does inclusion look like in your school?
- What did you learn from the case studies?
- What can you do to improve inclusive education in your school?

Resources and useful further reading

- Camden Award for Inclusion, Camden LA, London. Camden Award for Inclusion is a self-evaluation framework through which schools – primary, secondary, special and PRUs – assess the impact of their provision for pupils with Additional Educational Needs. Schools provide evidence and judgements for 28 'Quality Statements' in preparation for a one-day validation visit undertaken by a team of local authority inclusion consultants. The central aim of the process is to support school leaders in embedding sustainable practice. For further details, contact Neil Smith (neil.smith@camden.gov.uk).
- Inclusive Schools: Doorway booklet – inclusion and participation – provides top tips for inclusion and participation in sustainable schools.

- The National Strategies Four Quadrants Model – this model sets out the key actions leaders need to take to ensure effective leadership and management to narrow gaps in attainment and achievement between groups of pupils: FSM, G&T, SEN, Black and minority ethnic, gender.
- 'Pillars of Inclusion' Inclusive teaching and learning for pupils with SEN and/or disabilities – TDA Provides a useful checklist and evaluation tool for leaders seeking to ensure effective planning and teaching for pupils with SEN/disabilities.
- Inclusion Quality Mark – An award for inclusion established in the UK in October 2004 with the objective of supporting both state and independent schools to become truly inclusive.
- Brooks, G. (2007) *What Works Well for Children with Literacy Difficulties*. London: DfES – this is a DfES review of early intervention schemes that have been devised to help struggling readers and writers. It asks which schemes are used with children in Years 1 to 6 in the UK; what the schemes are like; and how effective each one is. Most of the schemes relate to the NLS 'third wave', that is, specifically targeted intervention for pupils identified as requiring SEN support.
- CLPE (The Centre for Literacy in Primary Education) (2012–2013). The Power of Reading Project. Available at: www.clpe.co.uk/research/power-of-reading
- DCSF (2008) *The Extra Mile: How Schools Succeed in Raising Aspirations in Deprived Communities*. Ref. no.: DCSF-00447-2008. London: DCSF.
- Department for Education (DfE) Narrowing the Gaps: Leadership for Impact. Available at: http://nationalstrategies.standards.dcsf.gov.uk/node/253660.
- Department for Education (DfE) Narrowing the Gaps: from Data Analysis to Impact: the Golden Thread. Available at: http://nationalstrategies.standards.dcsf.gov.uk/node/246991.
- Department for Education (DfE) Narrowing the Gaps: from Data Analysis to Impact: a Practical Guide. Available at: http://nationalstrategies.standards.dcsf.gov.uk/node/246822.
- Department for Education (DfE) Narrowing the Gaps: Resources to Support the Achievement of Black and Minority Ethnic, Disadvantaged and Gifted and Talented Pupils. Available at: http://nationalstrategies.standards.dcsf.gov.uk/node/227331?uc=force_uj
- Department for Education (DfE) A Strategy for Narrowing the Gaps. Available at: http://nationalstrategies.standards.dcsf.gov.uk/node/228340
- Department for Education (DfE) Gender and Achievement: Introduction and Key Issues. Available at: http://nationalstrategies.standards.dcsf.gov.uk/node/46134
- Department for Education (DfE) Ensuring the Attainment of Black Pupils. Available at: http://nationalstrategies.standards.dcsf.gov.uk/node/97328
- Dowker, A. (2004) *What Works Well for Children with Mathematical Difficulties: The Effectiveness of Interventions Schemes*. London: DfES. This is a DfES review of early intervention schemes that have been devised to help struggling pupils in maths.

References

Ainscow, M., Dyson, A., Booth, T. and Farrell, P. (2006) *Improving Schools, Developing Inclusion*. London: Routledge.

Bennett, P. (2010) A Special Achievement. *Leader Magazine*, The National College.

Black-Hawkins, K., Florian, L. and Rouse, M. (2007) *Achievement and Inclusion in Schools*. London: Routledge.

Booth, T. and Ainscow, M. (2000) *Index on Inclusion*. Bristol: Centre for Studies on Inclusive Education.

Davis, P. and Florian, L. (2004) *Teaching Strategies and Approaches for Pupils with Special Educational Needs: A Scoping Study*, DfES Research Report RR516. London: DfES.

Florian, L. and Black-Hawkins, K. (2010) Exploring Inclusive Pedagogy, *British Educational Research Journal* 37:5, p.14.

Frederickson, N. and Cline, T. (2009) *Special Educational Needs, Inclusion and Diversity: A Textbook*, 2nd edition (Chapters 3–4). Buckingham: Open University Press.

Fullan, M. (2001) *Leading in a Culture of Change*. San Francisco: Jossey-Bass.

Gibson, M. (2005) *Opportunities and Challenges: Additional Support for Learning (Scotland) Act 2004*. Paper delivered at a conference in Dublin by Mike Gibson, the Head of the Additional Support Needs Division in the Education Department of the Scottish Executive. Available at: www.nda.ie/cntmgmtnew.nsf/0/5D5B7CDA80DF742E802570A4005835E3/$File/Mike_Gibson_paper.doc [accessed 23 April 2009].

Greenhalgh, P. (1994) *Emotional Growth and Learning*. London: Routledge.

Kunc, N. (1992) The Need to Belong: Rediscovering Maslow's Hierarchy of Needs. In R. A. Villa, J. S. Thousand, W. Stainback and S. Stainback (eds), *Restructuring for Caring and Effective Schools*, pp. 25–39. Baltimore: Brooks.

Lawton, T. and Turnbull, T. (2007) *Inclusive Learning Approaches for Literacy, Language, Numeracy and ICT*. The Sector Skills Council for Lifelong Learning (LLUK).

Maslow, A. (1970) *Motivation and Personality*. New York: Harper & Row.

Rouse, M. (2008) *Developing Inclusive Practice: A Role for Teachers and Teacher Education?* Education in the North, 2008 – University of Aberdeen.

Warnock Report, The (1978) *Special Educational Needs*. London: HMSO.

Using Teacher-Led Research for School Improvement

Kim Insley

In this chapter, we will consider the following:

- What is action research?
- Self-evaluation: an unnecessary activity?
- Action research and teachers, teaching assistants and support staff
- Methodologies of action research
- Challenges of self-reflection and self-evaluation
- Setting up an action research project

This chapter will explore five aspects of teacher-led research by situating it in an action research paradigm. It also examines what action research is and, in the light of school self-evaluation, suggests that where teachers, teaching assistants and support staff know and understand the skills of the action researcher, they can then use these to improve outcomes for all learners. Each section examines action research elements and makes connections between practitioners and action researchers. The discussion is informed by exploration of case studies of practice in practitioner action research, particularly in the classroom and how this can further support the self-evaluation process. In doing so, the chapter identifies the value of knowing and understanding about action research methodologies for teaching professionals and other education support staff, and how the understanding of action research may impact on practice.

What is action research?

Action research is often described as practitioner research. It has a number of elements that are important within it but the relative importance of these elements depends on the researcher, the research question being examined and the expectations of outcomes. It has been described as

> ... *simply a form of self-reflective enquiry undertaken by participants in social situations in order to improve the rationality and justice of their own practices, their understanding of these practices, and the situations in which the practices are carried out.* (Carr and Kemmis, 1986: 162)

However, this description misses the opportunity of consideration about the outcomes of action research which often produce a change in both the teaching practice and the learners' engagement. Importantly, the practitioner is the active researcher whose reflection initiates the opportunity for change, such that new practices are introduced, which are again researched and may bring about further changes. Lewin identified this as the action research cycle which isn't just a circle of reflections identifying the need for change but more of a helix or spiral of steps. The first step is the identification of an initial idea, sometimes something that comes from a problem or a change (such as governmental decisions to change the curriculum) which leads to an audit of the information – a fact-finding exercise – followed by a planning stage. From the planning stage, the practitioner can identify the first action to be activated which is then evaluated and the plan amended. And so the cycle begins again with a second action. Rather than returning to the beginning of the cycle, the practitioner revisits the plan so that a piece of action research may come from a variety of cycles of action–plan–evaluate until a decision is made to finalise the research itself.

Another definition further supports this. Somekh (2006) states that action research:

> integrates research and action *in a series of flexible cycles involving, holistically rather than as separate steps: the collection of data about the topic of investigation; and analysis and interpretation of these data; the planning and introduction of action strategies to bring about positive changes; and evaluation of those changes through further data collection, analysis and interpretation ... and so forth to other flexible cycles until a decision is taken to intervene in this process in order to publish its outcomes to date.* (Somekh, 2006: 6, italics in original)

Action research project 1

Every term, the teachers at St Edward's Catholic Primary School[1] were expected to provide their plans for the head teacher so that he could monitor the teaching and learning going on in the school. This was accepted as 'normal' practice and in keeping with any regular expectation,

[1]Name of school changed to ensure confidentiality

different teachers provided different levels of plans. One teacher, new to the school, asked the head teacher how he knew that the plans he had received had been carried out. There was an expectation that teachers would make connections each term with the previous term's plans but this element of expectation had been eroded and it was clear that the head teacher knew what had been planned but not what had actually occurred. In completing the school's Self Evaluation Form (SEF) within the Ofsted framework, he recognized this. The senior management team (SMT) designed an action research project which enabled them to develop strategies across the school for the three different age groups (Foundation Stage, Key Stage 1 and Key Stage 2) and classes which worked in parallel (this was a two-form entry primary school), to reflect not just on the planned activities but the outcomes for learning from the planned teaching.

The action research elements of this project engaged the SMT in developing the research question and designing cycles of activity which enabled them to design the strategies (plan), implement them (do) and evaluate them (review). In sharing these with colleagues through the performance management system, new cycles of 'plan–do–review' were created. The SMT also acted as 'insider' researchers in that the action they planned was also implemented in their own practice.

Self-evaluation: an unnecessary activity?

The methodologies of action research include observation and reflection of practice and responses or behaviour associated with that practice. These will be further explored within the next section, but one important aspect which is pertinent to teaching is that, as action researchers, practitioners will also need to reflect on their own practice and behaviour. It is this reflection that further informs their understanding of why they do what they do, that is, reflexive practice. Before this reflexivity is achieved, it is important that researchers reflect on their own identity.

Activity 11.1: Who am I?

The starting point for considering your position is to consider why you do what you do. We are the way we are because of events in our lives – these can be called 'critical incidents' (Sikes et al., 2001). Critical incidents

(Continued)

(Continued)

often occur during periods of change and decision making. It is likely that personal critical phases such as marriage or divorce, birth or death of a close family member, or a partner's job move have affected your career patterns. Sikes et al. (2001: 104) identify three particular types of critical phase among teachers:

i   extrinsic
ii   intrinsic
iii personal

though these types can be identified within any career in education.

Create a timeline of your life by drawing a horizontal line, starting at the year you were born and marking on it every 10 years:

| 1957 | 1967 | 1977 | 1987 | 1997 | 2007 | 2011 |

Now add different incidents which may have affected you:

- in your family, e.g. moving house, the arrival of a new brother or sister
- in society at the time, e.g. a new government, a particular policy such as the increase in school age
- in school or university, e.g. staying on for A Levels, leaving home, a teacher or lecturer who inspired you
- in work places, e.g. a colleague, a new opportunity.

It is important within any action research about practice that knowledge and understanding of what researchers (who are also practitioners) bring is part of the reflexive engagement. This knowledge informs a clear understanding of identity, but it is also the understanding of how that identity is achieved that is important for the action researcher. These challenges are explored further in a later section. The initial stage in action research, which is self-reflection, benefits the later stages in the cycle.

Another important element of action research, which supports the reflexive activity, is the research journal. This is where the researcher records observations, discussions, field notes, responses to planned action and reflections on outcomes; it forms the 'raw' data of the researcher. This important document can be likened to teachers' record books or 'day books' and is often used to inform feedback to senior management, governor, local authority (LA) advisers and the head teacher on what actually happens in the classroom.

Action research project 2

A secondary (Key Stages 3 and 4) history teacher has identified a research question which asks about the value of encouraging her pupils to understand assessment activity outcomes. She keeps records of the pupils' scores for each element, colour coding them to identify her concerns: red for limited learning, yellow for some development and green for the pupil being on target to achieve expected grades at the end of the school year. Her research journal records discussions with the pupils on how they feel about the colour coding (among other discussions) and by grouping and matching comments she began to see patterns in her pupils' responses. These patterns allowed her to develop questions to inform further 'action' in her project: group interviews. Her project, when completed, demonstrates an increase in achievement for all pupils in her tutor group and, in comparing with the parallel tutor group, a significant difference in achievements. Her report to the Head of Humanities is taken to the governing body with a recommendation from the senior team that all teachers use a similar strategy.

Action research and teachers, teaching assistants and support staff

Teaching has a whole range of practices and activities which may vary according to local practices and customs. Strategies for teaching can range from a transmission model where knowledge is identified as the most important aspect of education to a fully interactive model where the teacher is only a facilitator who enables the learner in managing and leading their own learning and all the dimensions of teaching within.

Activity 11.2: What is teaching?

Choose a clean sheet of paper and put the word 'teaching' in the middle and, using a word association technique, write down on separate 'Post-it' notes words or phrases that come to mind when you think of teaching.

When you have completed these, rearrange the words, grouping those that go together, and see if you can 'name' the groups. When different groups have done this, they have come up with groups of words within Assessment, Telling, Facilitating and Learning.

Twenty years ago, Alexander (1992) challenged the UK primary teaching establishment when he explored the concept of practice. He identified practice as having at least four other considerations. The concept includes skills and understanding (as well as knowledge) and can be explored through a collective understanding of teaching. However, Alexander then situates that conceptual consideration by highlighting *political* and *pragmatic* elements which by themselves reflect 'practice: a minimal definition' (Alexander, 1992: 190) and *value* and *empirical* elements. All five elements or considerations – Conceptual, Pragmatic, Political, Value and Empirical – offer a model for 'good practice' which might have elements of readers' understanding of the concept.

In relation to action research, it may be considered that the questions Alexander asks with regard to each concept are similar to those that the action researcher might ask. This can be highlighted by looking at his Empirical Considerations:

> *Do I actually have the evidence that the practice I am commending or adopting promotes learning? What kind of evidence? My own experience? Research findings? Am I prepared to allow for the possibility that there might be contrary evidence? Am I prepared to allow for the empirical perspective or am I going to press my view of good practice regardless? (Alexander, 1992: 186–187)*

An excellent example of the developments within teaching as being the outcomes of action research can be examined when considering assessment. Assessment plays an important part in teaching and we now have reflection on assessment *for* learning, or formative assessment, as well as assessment *of* learning, or summative assessment (Assessment Reform Group, 1999). Both assessment processes have an important part to play in teaching, although it is formative assessment or Assessment *for* Learning which can be most like action research in its reflective and informative elements. However, Burton et al. liken action research to the assessment processes teachers employ at the end-of-year or summative assessment: '... action research generates findings *for* practice (informing practice) as well as *of* practice (research report)' (2008: 125). Action research projects which are undertaken in classrooms, such as that described in project 2 above, often include elements of assessment.

Good teachers are reflective practitioners (Schon, 1991; Pollard, 2008) and this reflection matches action research methodologies already described and others which form part of the teaching or practice concept.

Methodologies of action research

It is important to recognize that an understanding of identity and how that identity is achieved is one element of methodology of action research. It helps establish the area of practice to be explored, informing research questions and the 'plan' stage of the research cycle. Having identified the research question, researchers will be able to identify how they will explore it. There is a range of methodologies available but those reflecting 'practice' are often preferred by the action researcher. A good practitioner will use observation, questioning and assessment to improve teaching. These are also recognized methodologies of qualitative research but to be more than good teaching and effective research methodologies, there needs to be a framework within the planning which enables the researcher to reflect back on the plan stage, that is 'review'. The 'do' stage of the cycle involves action developed from the 'plan' and/or 'review' stages, thus reflecting Lewin's helix described earlier.

Observations are often part of normal teacher activity, especially part of formative assessment processes. In research, if observation is considered a valid form of collection of data (and many action researchers use it particularly where the participants may not be able to engage in discussion, questionnaires or interview activities), then developing an observation framework can support the rigour of the data collection method. This framework can be set around time (watch for 5 minutes, write for 5 minutes) or language (record speech and interactions including non-verbal engagement) or behaviour (recording what a participant actually does, avoiding emotive language which may reflect the researcher's feelings and emotions rather than the participant's behaviour). Repeated observations help establish the validity of findings, especially where it is possible to identify repeated outcomes. It is also possible to support observation data with video recordings and photographs. The analysis of observation data can help establish hypotheses, develop themes to be explored or identify a better focus to be examined, so through the 'review' stage move on within the helix to a new 'plan' stage.

Action research project 3

A nursery teacher chose observation to help her explore how parents could help their children learn to read. The common practice in the school was to send home books for sharing with the children, but there seemed to be little effect on children's engagement with books. Having shared with parents at a meeting (supported by the head teacher and Foundation Stage Coordinator) the reasons for sending home books and asking parents to read with their children, talking about how this could help and identifying strategies to do so, the researcher set up parent–children afternoons when parents came into the nursery and read with their children. She observed their practice and, in working with parents who agreed to be included in the research, she was able to share with them how their children engaged with them when they read together and so identify ways forward.

The use of semi or informal interviews, discussions and engagements with participants in the research group is another methodology which is a valuable data source. Again, framing the questions or area for discussion is important but importantly, researchers do not ask their research question. The research question needs to be situated and areas around it explored. These explorations help identify the investigation around the research question. Within action research, group interviews are often a useful methodology where the researcher is also a member of the discussion, leading participants towards discussion of the action being examined. In action research, the methodologies of qualitative research which use questioning will be focused on discussion and investigating the action or 'do' stage, including 'reviewing', so identifying other actions on the helix of action research.

Many action researchers use questionnaires to explore their participants' starting point, but in practice these often do not give enough valid information as it is recognized that the development of a research questionnaire is important and this is a whole research area to be explored (but not here).

Challenges of self-reflection and self-evaluation

Earlier on in this chapter, the importance of identity was established within the action research paradigm. A major challenge for the practitioners is that of the 'insider' action researcher. In considering their own practices, it can be argued, the researcher loses the objectivity important in research to give it validity and reliability. In order to achieve this objectivity, part of the reflections in the helix of steps should include an examination of what the researcher practitioner brings to the investigation. Biography as an element of the examination of the setting in which the research is situated has been established through much research practice, including the development from anthropology of ethnographic research methodologies. Where practitioners reflect on their journey to being a teacher (in a similar way to that begun in Activity 11.1), knowing what has moulded their identity as a teacher, then planning the research acknowledges and accepts the practitioner bias, allowing the knowledge to inform the collection of data. The insider has knowledge that the outsider cannot necessarily access, but this knowledge must be examined and considered.

Action research project 4

Sara,[2] a music teacher at an international secondary school in Europe, was amazed to realize that a critical incident for her development into a music teacher was when she joined a choir at the age of 7. In reflecting

[2]Name has been changed to preserve anonymity

on her teaching, she was now certain that it was her love of singing which influenced her choice of music for her pupils to listen to. In considering the change element within her own action research project, this critical incident became important in her planning of the research and the research question she developed. Her first action was to change the music which pupils listened to, choosing the International Baccalaureate suggested range, but then she recognized that her bias was actually a positive element in helping pupils engage. Her reflection identified a new action, to use group discussion and semi-structured interviews to identify a wider range of appropriate music which her pupils were motivated about. This increased the range and, following further review, the teacher changed teaching strategies so that her pupils introduced the music to their colleagues. The outcomes of this small piece of action research were measured in the aural examinations at the end of the year, demonstrating an increase in achievements as well as pupils having a positive response to a range of music.

Another element of action research could be the recognition of co-researchers. Other practitioners who work with the researcher become researchers in their own right. Some suggest that all action research should be collaborative (Kemmis and McTaggart, 2005) by its very nature of examining ongoing practice, and this collaboration may be a regular part of teams of teachers working together in a school developing a learning community, not just for their pupils or students but also for themselves.

Action research project 5

The head teacher of a successful primary school rated 'outstanding' in the last three inspections carried out by Ofsted, was concerned that she had no more strategies for continuing the outstanding practices in the school. She was satisfied that new staff joining were engaged and responded appropriately to the activities and strategies which resulted in positive outcomes, but continuing staff were less motivated. The opportunity to teach all staff (including teaching assistants and support staff) arose and following five training sessions every three weeks during one term, staff worked together to identify action research projects. Some staff worked in teaching teams: the foundation stage staff identified a project on developing parent meetings; the Key Stage 2 staff worked together on a project to explore improvements in maths teaching across the upper key stage (children aged 9, 10 and 11 years).

(Continued)

(Continued)

Support staff worked with the head teacher to develop playground activities. Some staff worked in pairs: the administration/office staff identified the challenges of improving unauthorized absence figures, developing a note-writing scheme for parents; a teacher and her teaching assistant investigated strategies for supporting their 6-year-olds in writing stories. Four individuals chose their own projects which they completed as part of their MA research projects. All projects were recorded and groups, pairs and individuals presented outcomes in written reports or oral reports for the governing body.

This leads to self-evaluation as the co-researchers evaluate elements of their research. The 'review' stage is vital in the development of the action research as, without these cycles, Lewin's developmental helix is not achieved. However, the challenge of self-evaluation is that the action research seems never-ending. The action researcher and co-researchers never reach a conclusion. To help, it is suggested that the project is given a boundary (explored in the next section).

Setting up an action research project

The challenge for any practitioner in setting up an action research project is often focusing the research question. Earlier in the chapter, the suggestion was that the researcher should situate the research question but experience suggests that this is one of the more difficult aspects of the action research project. The action researcher who is a practitioner and an 'insider' researcher must somehow detach from the other practices that will be occurring at the same time as the action research. It is easier to achieve this if the initial elements of the research are completed, including reflection on identity. Establishing the research question and the boundaries of that research question are the next stage.

Activity 11.3: What am I interested in?

Action research texts often have excellent suggestions for identifying starting points (see further reading list). This activity has been used by many practitioners to help them focus ideas.

Write a paragraph about what it is you are interested in. Do not spend time thinking – time yourself (take only 15 minutes) and just write. When the 15 minutes is over, finish the sentence you are on and then take a highlighter and identify the key words within your paragraph.

These words may be nouns, adjectives, verbs or adverbs but they will be key words which are important in your practice. You might be able to group these words, list them in order of priority and identify things which are more 'red herrings', sending you off in the wrong direction. Do this and then choose no more than five key words for your research. Form these into a question ... this is your research question.

The simple 'plan–do–review' mantra helps identify the steps within the helix of action research. Whether the researcher works with others, in their own setting or in a related setting (such as a colleague's classroom), the boundaries of action research are important to establish. Many practitioners do this by identifying just what it is they are not going to research. These may be finalized as other research projects, but clarifying just what is to be researched is important.

Conclusion

Teachers who are good practitioners and engage in reflective and reflexive practice in considering their work are already working within an action research paradigm. Other members of the school society, teaching assistants, support staff and even pupils can also be action researchers or co-researchers. The elements of action research are similar to those of the effective practitioner. The action research project offers an opportunity for all practitioners in school to impact on practice by exploring their practice using the rigorous and valid activities of the action researcher. The outcomes will change practice and enable self-reflection and self-evaluation to be achieved.

Questions for further thinking

- What do you think is the value of action research?
- Are there any key questions that you would be interested in researching?
- How should action research be disseminated?

Resources and useful further reading

Hopkins, D. (2008) *A Teacher's Guide to Action Research*. Maidenhead: OUP – a clear description on how to conduct classroom research, with good chapters on analysing and organizing research.

McNiff, J. and Whitehead, J. (2005) *Action Research for Teachers: A Practical Guide*. London: David Fulton Publishers – a very practical guide.

References

Alexander, R. (1992) *Policy and Practice in Primary Education*. London: Routledge.

Assessment Reform Group (1999) *Assessment for Learning: Beyond the Black Box*. Cambridge: University of Cambridge School of Education.

Burton, N., Brundrett, M. and Jones, M. (2008) *Doing Your Education Research Project*. London: Sage.

Carr, W. and Kemmis, S. (1986) *Becoming Critical: Education, Knowledge and Action Research*. Lewes: Falmer.

Kemmis, S. and McTaggart, R. (2005) Participatory Action Research, in N. Denzin and Y. Lincoln (eds) *Handbook of Qualitative Research*, 3rd edition, pp. 559–604. London: Sage.

Pollard, A. (ed.) (2008) *Reflective Teaching: Evidence-informed Professional Practice*, 3rd edition. London: Continuum.

Schon, D. (ed.) (1991) *The Reflective Turn: Case Studies in and on Educational Practice*. London: Teachers College Press.

Sikes, P., Measor, L. and Woods, P. (2001) Critical Phases and Incidents, in J. Solar, A. Craft and H. Burgess (eds) *Teacher Development: Exploring Our Own Practice*. London: Paul Chapman Publishing.

Somekh, B. (2006) *Action Research: A Methodology for Change and Development*. Maidenhead: Open University Press.

Part III
Looking Outwards

Preparing for Ofsted

Barbara and Graham Saltmarsh

In this chapter, we will consider the following:

- A brief history of Ofsted to date
- An overview of the Ofsted Framework and Evaluation Schedule
- What realistically can be done before Ofsted descend
- Some things that you need to be prepared for
- Before the inspectors arrive
- The inspection begins
- An Inspector Calls
- Every Child Matters (ECM)

With clipboard under arm, the inspector opened the Year 6 classroom door and strode in with the customary suitable look of authority. The inspector hadn't reckoned on the immensely likeable boy from a local Traveller family; let's call him Noah Trotter. Noah commenced to loudly and loyally tell his teacher 'Oh, Oh, look out Miss, Oxfam have just arrived!' With that, both teacher and inspector collapsed with laughter; the ice was broken. It was a great lesson.

The object of this chapter is to enable you to do the same – in other words, to prepare and deliver outstanding lessons not just for the benefit of some itinerant here today, gone tomorrow Ofsted inspector but to establish the confident and competent good practice they look for but also as the norm in your classroom.

A brief history of Ofsted to date

Ofsted is an acronym for The Office for Standards in Education and Children's Services and Skills. It is one of the most wide-ranging and powerful so-called quangos. It was formed in 1992 and an early HM Chief Inspector was Chris Woodhead whose robust views on school standards and of teachers in particular were not always well received by the education establishment of the day. Its role was to bring together what were seen as variable local inspection regimes and introduce a national framework of school standards which became the criteria for all schools to aspire to. All schools were then routinely inspected approximately every three years unless they were deemed as failing when the inspection periods became increasingly concentrated and rigorous. The main inspection outcome categories were then Excellent, Very Good, Good, Satisfactory or Unsatisfactory. A failing school would be deemed as needing 'Special Measures', a category that is still current today. Prior to September 2005, schools were inspected across a week and were given two months' notice to prepare for an inspection. This system fell into disrepute. It disrupted schools for a prolonged period leading up to the inspection and the inspection itself may not have revealed the true character of the school.

Most school inspections are carried out by so-called 'Additional Inspectors' (AI). They are employed by external companies known as 'Inspection Service Providers' (ISPs). Currently, almost all AIs have teaching experience at a senior level, except for a few who have been retained from the previous regime in which each inspection team included a 'Lay Inspector', a role that was abolished some years ago.

The majority of inspections of secondary schools and sixth-form colleges are led by one of Her Majesty's Inspectors of Schools supported by a team of AIs. Most inspection visits of schools deemed to be failing in some way are also HMI led. In the main, primary school inspections are led by a suitably qualified AI. These are now known as *Section 5 Inspections*, referring to the section in the legislation that sets out the inspection process. Currently, schools are categorised as being Outstanding, Good, Satisfactory or Inadequate.

From September 2009, outstanding or good schools may be inspected after five years rather than three years. This depends on the results of a risk assessment process carried out in the third year after the last inspection. In order to assist in deciding whether Ofsted could wait longer than three years before undertaking a full inspection of a good or outstanding school, Her Majesty's Inspectors will consider various sources of information about the school's performance. This is called an 'interim assessment'.

The 2011 Education Bill proposed that, from January 2012, schools that were previously judged to be outstanding would not be subject to routine inspection unless concerns were raised about their performance. Again, this would involve Ofsted carrying out an initial risk assessment to see if the school concerned warrants an inspection.

An interim assessment will take into account the following:

- pupils' attainment – including the attainment of significant groups of pupils, with a focus on pupils identified with SEN, and pupils' attainment in core subjects
- pupils' progress – including the progress made by different groups of pupils
- pupils' attendance
- any inspection visits carried out by Ofsted since the last section 5 inspection
- any qualifying complaints about the school made by parents or carers
- any other significant issues brought to Ofsted's attention, for example by the local authority.

From 2012, the routine inspection framework will have undergone significant changes but will still take account of the school's own self-evaluation evidence and particularly take into account the views of parents and carers in deciding when schools should be inspected. The government has declared that there will be a more rigorous scrutiny of behaviour and that inspections will be targeted to bring about a more rapid improvement in schools judged to be inadequate.

An overview of the Ofsted Framework and Evaluation Schedule

Ofsted states that the purpose of a school inspection is to provide an independent external evaluation of its effectiveness and a diagnosis of what it should do to improve, based upon a range of evidence including that from first-hand observation. Ofsted's school inspection reports present a written commentary on the outcomes achieved and the quality of the school's provision (especially the quality of teaching and its impact on learning), the effectiveness of leadership and management and the school's capacity to improve.

These school inspections perform three essential functions. They:

- provide parents/carers with information which informs their choices and preferences about the effectiveness of the schools their children attend or may go to
- keep the Secretary of State (and parliament) informed about the work of schools. This provides assurance that minimum standards are being met; provides confidence in the use of public money; and assists accountability
- promote the improvement of individual schools and the education system as a whole.

At the time of writing, Ofsted is conducting a consultation process on a revised school inspection framework. There will be four key areas covering teaching, behaviour, leadership and achievement. It will test, evaluate and discuss aspects of the framework with some schools prior to implementation and there will be an extensive programme of pilot inspections. Obviously, the views of inspectors will also be taken into account as to the practical application of some proposals.

It is already certain that 'Good' and 'Outstanding' schools will be assessed by data analysis every three years. Outstanding schools will not be routinely inspected and Good schools only every five years; but an inspection can in future be triggered by a parental complaint via Ofsted's website. Indeed, under the new framework any school can itself request an inspection if it is prepared to pay for the privilege. It is not expected that this will get a huge take-up! Can you visualise a school paying for an inspection only then to be put into a category?

It is believed that there will be a reduced bias towards pupil safety which has caused a number of headaches for schools and occasionally has gone beyond the bounds of common sense. The proposals for change are not controversial in themselves and should address some of the previous concerns that schools, teachers and their professional bodies have reasonably expressed. But it is understood that the emphasis on behaviour will include interviews with pupils who may have been the victims of bullying.

However, although some aspects such as spiritual, moral, social and cultural development may take a back seat, it would be wrong to assume that these important features of a school will in future be disregarded. In the same way, it is expected that Community Cohesion as a specific aspect may well be dropped. This is to be welcomed because its loose definition has caused difficulty for schools and inspectors alike. Primary schools, in particular, have always had difficulty in fully complying with its prescriptive definition.

Inspectors are expected to spend more time in the classroom giving attention to pupils' attainment and rates of progress. Inspectors will return to the practice of listening to primary school pupils reading.

From 2012, the main proposals for the inspection framework are likely to include:

- a report on the quality of the education provided by the school, giving priority to the achievement of its pupils and their behaviour and safety, the quality of teaching and the quality of leadership and management of the school
- the spiritual, moral, social and cultural development of pupils and the extent to which the education provided enables every pupil to achieve their potential, particularly disabled pupils and those with special educational needs
- being far more streamlined with even greater emphasis on and detailed observation of teaching and learning
- taking particular account of pupils' attainment and rates of progress when evaluating achievement
- focusing strongly on standards of reading and numeracy in primary schools and literacy in secondary schools

- measures of relative progress other than contextual value-added indicators
- more emphasis on reporting on pupil behaviour, with particular attention paid to conduct in lessons and around the school. Pupil safety and freedom from bullying and harassment will be taken into account
- focusing on evaluating the quality of teaching and the use of assessment to support effective learning
- evaluating how well reading is taught in primary schools and how well literacy is taught in secondary schools
- the effectiveness of leadership and management, especially the leadership of teaching and learning
- the overall effectiveness of the school by giving more weight to the quality of teaching and pupils' achievement, their behaviour and the impact of leadership and management, including how well the school promotes the spiritual, moral, social and cultural development of pupils
- a report on the effectiveness of sixth-form and early years provision within the other reporting areas, rather than separate sections as is current practice.

In future, Ofsted will give greater attention to requests to inspect because of some concern about a particular school. Requests for inspection may relate to concerns about a school's performance; this may relate to behaviour or a decline in test and examination results. Such requests may come from groups of parents, a local authority or the governing body.

The evaluation schedule sets out the judgements inspectors will make across a range of aspects and, along with the framework, can be accessed in full at the Ofsted website. Inspectors are required to weigh up the balance of evidence in a particular area and consider it against the descriptors for outstanding, good, satisfactory or inadequate before making a judgement. It is essential that inspectors use grade descriptors and the associated outline guidance against the context of the school being inspected. Schools are increasingly prepared to challenge inspectors where they feel that judgements are flawed because inspectors may have missed the bigger picture and this is where the school's senior management must be prepared to provide additional evidence to support their challenge.

What realistically can be done before Ofsted descend

Remember that, at the moment, you have two days' notice. Most of what we mention here should be in place in school as good practice anyway. There are some quick wins you can ensure that you have in place which will help the inspectors and also smooth your passage through the actual inspection.

Good practice (hopefully already in place, it's worth remembering that inspectors can smell wet paint!):

- a stimulating and well-organised learning environment
- relevant, recent and interactive displays
- targets and learning walls displayed
- resources organised to ensure independent learning and that all pupils' needs are supported
- work marked and up to date. Marking should follow school marking policy and show next steps and evidence that the pupil has acted on the (age-appropriate) marking comments
- lesson plans which indicate, among other things, differentiation, assessment for learning opportunities and, where appropriate, deployment of support staff
- knowledge of what your subject looks like across the school (if you are a curriculum leader). Where are the strengths and areas for development? Be clear on how you gain insight into your curriculum area, i.e. from lesson observations, learning walks and work scrutiny. Be familiar with the data on your area if it is shown in RAISEonline. Know how different groups of pupils are progressing (Every Child Matters). Are there any particular groups who are doing well or underachieving?
- pupils knowing their targets and what their next steps are.

Some quick wins

Remember that you will have, at the most, two days before the inspection starts. So the following are what, realistically, you can do when you first hear that the inspection will take place:

- **DON'T PANIC!** If the above good practice is in place, you should feel confident.
- **Get the SLT to prepare some things in advance.** There are some organisational things that the senior leadership should address, apart from the school evaluation data in whichever form that is. Ofsted can access this online, as well as the school's last Ofsted report and RAISEonline. Although the School Evaluation Form (SEF) has never been statutory, the need for a school to review and evaluate is. So how can the SLT assist inspectors? Provision of the following are appreciated:
  - maps so that the inspectors don't get lost!
  - timetables for the inspection period
  - staff lists, class lists and roles and responsibilities
  - a place to work (that is bigger than a cupboard), tables and adult-sized chairs
  - access to electricity points
  - refreshments – these are always appreciated and say a lot about how your school treats visitors
  - data that is sign-posted with Post-it notes so that information is easily found. Time is of the essence

o making sure all staff are aware of the issues that have arisen from the pre- inspection briefing (PIB). These will be the trails and foci the inspection will be following across the school.

What you as a classroom practitioner can do

- Provide a seating plan for your class and list of who is in the class, e.g. SEND, EAL and FSM, gender balance.
- Clarify the number on role in your class and the number present at that lesson. This can be put in the corner of the white board.
- Ensure it is clear in your plans exactly who (if any) support staff are supporting and the interventions they are included in. Really, this next bit of advice should come into good practice: ensure that support staff know what the lesson objectives are and their role in them. Try and avoid your support staff sitting on the carpet unengaged with the lesson. This is never a good idea and inspectors will comment on the deployment of support staff.
- Make sure you have two seats (adult seats are appreciated) to cater for any joint inspections and observations.
- Prepare your class for visitors. Inspectors appreciate a smile and a welcome.
- Ensure the temperature of the classroom is conducive to learning.
- Ensure lesson plans and the information mentioned above is on the chairs provided for the inspectors (have several copies in case they walk off with them!).
- Avoid deciding to run an integrated day if you have never taught in that way. The first day of your inspection is not the best time to experiment with being too clever or taking risks that you have never taken before. Having said that, do make sure your lessons are pacey and exciting. It can be a temptation to play it too safe.
- Remember that it is the curriculum that engages the pupil and that this is what will help you with behaviour management – 40 minutes on the carpet and 5 minutes on independent work may not help you take control of the class. Conduct in class and around the school is an important focus of the new framework.
- Never be afraid to stop a lesson if you feel that you need to. Try to be as normal as possible. None of us likes being inspected and, remember, inspectors can feel nervous too!

Some things that you need to be prepared for

Joint observations are done by an inspector and one of your SLT, most usually the head teacher. These are to validate the school judgements of teaching and learning. The feedback, should you want it, is given by the senior leader.

Inspectors will normally stay for 30 minutes, during this time they will talk to children and look at work. If an inspector stays at least 20 minutes, you will be entitled to feedback at some point in the day. It will be up to you to seek out the inspector to get your feedback.

In a large school, not everyone will be seen teaching although inspectors do their very best to see as many lessons as possible.

If you are a curriculum leader, SENCO, FLO, EAL teacher, for example, you will most likely have a discussion with an inspector. Do not feel you have to do everything from memory – you may take what data you need but please be familiar with it.

Before the inspectors arrive

The lead inspector (LI) will have a telephone conversation with your head teacher and they will discuss the PIB. This will be drawn up by the LI using the school data that is available online, i.e. SEF, RAISEonline and the previous inspection report.

Through this analysis of the school data and discussion with the head teacher, the main inspection foci will emerge. You should make yourself aware of what those foci are.

The inspection begins

When your school is being inspected by Ofsted, it goes without saying that it is a stressful time for the entire school community. However, you won't be the only ones. The inspectors themselves will be under considerable time constraints to organise themselves. Rarely are members of the inspection team local to your school. More likely, they will have travelled some distance and they may not be alive to local issues or events that have had an impact on the school. They will often have found themselves accommodation nearby and they may not even know each other. The school will have been provided with a brief profile of each inspector with details of their particular area of expertise or specialism. For example, some inspectors have strong specialist subject skills or early years/sixth form experience. They will, of course, read the school's own self-evaluation but that may not necessarily convey everything they need to know and that is why the LI will continue to have a close working relationship with your head teacher throughout the entire event. The majority of inspections take place over two working school days but some of the inspectors may only be present for one day, normally day one. The size of the inspection team is decided by the number of children on the school roll. So, for example, at a one-form entry primary, there is only likely to be two inspectors and one of those may be leaving at the end of day one. Large secondary schools will of course have much larger teams.

From the point of view of the inspectors, the day starts at 8.00 a.m. The school will have offered the team a suitable room to use as a base, although in very small village schools this has been known to comprise the top of a piano in the hall! Inspectors can regale you with many curious stories of the places they have been and worked at, ranging from caravans to a bit of the village hall and even presbyteries! The LI and the head teacher will have agreed to take a whistle-stop tour of the school so that everyone can familiarise themselves with the layout. Inspectors are human beings, they know how stressful this is for you and the advantage of the current framework is that of working *with* the school to see it at its best. So don't be afraid to introduce yourself and talk with them, as it will be appreciated. Also, tell the children to be open and helpful; most inspectors find their way around unfamiliar schools by using the children as guides. It is accepted protocol that at no time will inspectors go into or use the staff room unless specifically asked in; you need some point of refuge!

After the tour, there will be a brief introduction to the entire staff – at this time, the LI will explain the process for your particular school and should tell you when the team will be available to give you feedback on lessons they have attended. Then the inspection team will have its own meeting. Each inspector will already have been notified as to what aspects of the inspection they will be responsible for and these will follow the framework. For example, one of the team may have responsibility for safeguarding and care guidance and support, but between meetings with key staff they will still be expected to get into lessons which may have been divided up in year groups or by subject. The school will have provided the team with timetables, data, policy documents and much more besides.

By lunchtime on day one, the team will briefly re-meet and may have already formed a very provisional view on some aspects of the school, for example behaviour. The head teacher will be invited to attend all meetings and it is at these times that the school may wish – or be requested – to provide additional evidence, for example a trawl through the books of a particular year group to look at marking, standards of handwriting/work or whatever the team think will help it to reach a judgement on a particular aspect. There will be a similar meeting at the conclusion of day one and by then some more firm but still provisional judgements may have been arrived at.

The inspection activity normally concludes by lunchtime on day two. There will then be a final meeting, attended by the head teacher, when all of the inspection grades for each aspect will be finalised. Later that day, the results of the inspection findings will be fed back to the senior leaders, governors and possibly a representative from the local authority. The LI's report will then be edited and, finally, published within a week to 10 days.

An Inspector Calls

An inspector will have a focus for the classroom observation. This will be taken from the PIB. *This is why it is important that the PIB is shared and that points for the inspection are known.*

It could be that a focus is differentiation within a lesson. This, of course, will be shown on your lesson plans and reflected in the resources available and the way in which you use any support you have in the class. Sometimes, if the data has shown that there is a particular group of pupils who are underachieving across the school or in a particular cohort, this will be a focus.

The inspector will also speak to pupils and ask questions about their learning within the lesson. An example of this was overheard in a reception class, where the children were doing some work on floating and sinking. A boy was testing various materials and, when asked, was able to say and demonstrate that wood floated. When asked about the metal objects, he said very confidently, 'they sink'. The inspector put a pin on the surface of the water which floated. 'Why do you think that happened?' There was a long pause. Then, not to be caught out, our cunning 5-year-old said, 'Do you want to see my new vest?'

The pace of a lesson is always of interest to inspectors, along with the impact on progress that is made by all groups of pupils, and whether pupils are aware of their targets and what they need to do to reach them or in fact even have any.

How does behaviour impact on learning outcomes? Is there a lot of low-level disruption? Remember, never be afraid to stop a lesson if you feel that pupils are taking advantage of having visitors in the room. This is why it is important to prepare your class for the coming inspection. Do not hype it up as that is only asking for trouble. Explain that we want people to see us learning at our best. It can be a good idea when the inspector appears at your door to welcome them and briefly say what the lesson is about or indeed ask a 'reliable' pupil to tell them.

The inspector, broadly speaking, will look for evidence in the following areas:

- attainment
- learning and progress, taking into account the learning and progress of different groups of pupils in coming to their overall judgement
- behaviour
- teaching
- assessment to support learning
- curriculum
- care, guidance and support
- aspects of ECM (see below).

And, if there is enough evidence, they will grade them: (1) Outstanding, (2) Good, (3) Satisfactory or (4) Inadequate.

You can make yourself familiar with the grade descriptors by looking on the Ofsted website and reading the relevant parts of the Framework.

Remember, when you are receiving your feedback, it is an opportunity to ask 'What do I need to do to be even better or improve?' Don't be afraid to explain why you took a particular course of action during the lesson. You know your pupils while the inspector does not.

Every Child Matters (ECM)

Every Child Matters became the government's vision for all children's services and was published in September 2003. It followed on from the tragic death of Victoria Climbié who was abused and murdered in her own home by her guardians despite the local social services being aware of her circumstances. This led to a public enquiry which resulted in major changes in every aspect of child protection. In September 2003, this reshaping of children's services was designed to achieve five key outcomes for children and young people:

- Be healthy
- Stay safe
- Enjoy and achieve
- Make a positive contribution
- Achieve economic wellbeing

This was followed by legislation (The Children Act 2004) which has since formed the basis of a long-term programme of change in the way children's services work together. Ofsted have embraced all of these concepts, not only by practising them in all they do but naturally also by vigorously scrutinising how well schools and other settings are working to these minimum standards of care for children and young people.

So far as school inspections are concerned, Ofsted will take an overall holistic view on outcomes for pupils, such as feelings of safety, pupils' behaviour and the extent to which they adopt healthy lifestyles. Evidence for these aspects will also be drawn from pupil and parental questionnaires which will have been sent out just prior to the inspection visit. A significant amount of inspection time is dedicated to assessing the effectiveness of safeguarding procedures and this aspect is what is classed as a *limiting judgement* – in other words, if the school fails in this one aspect alone, it cannot expect anything other than to be placed in a category for immediate rectification. In other words, it can fail if this single aspect is deemed inadequate. Do check the framework for the criteria applied to safeguarding and you will note how comprehensive it is.

In the classroom, you can make a significant contribution as to how these aspects are applied to your school overall. Every inspector that visits your classroom will note their observations and assessments on a standard evidence form, colloquially known as an EF. At the foot of each EF is a section asking inspectors for particular evaluations that are directly in line with the Every Child Matters criteria. These cover safety, health, contribution to the community, economic wellbeing and the extent of pupils' spiritual, moral, social and cultural development (SMSC).

It is not our place in this section to dictate to teachers what should or should not be included in each lesson. Indeed, if you at any one time tried to embrace every ECM concept in, say, a maths lesson, it would look ridiculous and will be spotted as such.

But obviously, first and foremost, you must ensure that your classroom or setting for the lesson is a safe place for everybody. Be alive to health and safety issues and the possible need for overall risk assessments to have been put in place, say, for example, in science and PE lessons. Behaviour is an obvious aspect for safety.

Inspectors really appreciate watching real-life learning in action so by cross-referencing your teaching you can automatically help the inspector note that your class is looking at their health and economic wellbeing. In the same way, by celebrating our natural world, its human diversity and traditions, it will be clear you are noting aspects of SMSC. In fact, you can have a lot of productive fun by embracing and including part or sometimes all of these areas within your lesson, and SMSC is certainly a component which goes to make some lessons truly outstanding.

Conclusion

Remember that most Ofsted inspectors have a background steeped in school leadership. They will often have visited literally hundreds of schools across their career. First impressions certainly count, but don't go overboard. Never make the mistake of trying to characterise your school as something that it isn't; instead always play to your strengths. For example, at one school visited a few years ago, as the inspectors entered the reception area they were confronted with an inflatable child's paddling pool full of water, right in front of the receptionist's counter. One of the inspectors tripped and his foot went in a full eight inches of cold water as he steadied himself, asking in fairly expletive terms what it was doing there. A flustered head teacher emerged from his office, explaining to the inspectors and several sniggering pupils that it was the school's 'pool of tranquillity'. It wasn't a great start to the inspection.

Questions for further thinking

- A good way of reviewing the way you want to present your school is to imagine that you are an inspector walking into your reception area for the first time; what would you be looking for?
- What is the first thing that would get noticed or, more to the point, what is it that you *want* to be noticed?
- What do the displays/notice boards say about your school?

- Is there something on display that makes your values and vision explicit?
- Does your school convey a sense of community? For example, do you have club and school council notice boards, information about governors and a parent notice board?
- Are visitors greeted in a professional but warm and friendly manner?
- Do you ensure that the school's safeguarding policy in respect of all visitors is fully complied with, i.e. signing in, visitor ID and any evacuation/fire procedures?

Inside and around the school

- Imagine that the inspector is on a 'learning walk' – what are they going to see?
- Is the school clean and tidy with no litter or graffiti?
- Are the toilets clean?
- What are the attitudes and behaviour of pupils like?
- Are stairs, corridors and landings well supervised at busy times?
- Are exits clearly marked and unobstructed?
- Is signage good and can visitors find their way around easily?
- Is your health and safety policy being complied with?
- What is the seating and shelter like in the playground?
- Playground markings – are they bright or faded?

Your classrooms

- Do your classrooms have a commonality of 'house style'?
- Are your classrooms well organised and preparing pupils to be independent learners?
- Are your classrooms user-friendly for pupils who may have barriers to overcome in their learning and activities?
- Does everything work (e.g. IT, interactive white boards, clocks, etc.)?
- Is there sufficient space to facilitate the transition between group and individual work?
- Have you removed broken/damaged furniture, together with any faulty equipment? (This is especially important in an early years setting.)
- Are your heating and ventilation systems adequate?
- Have you made space for visitors?
- Are pupils' books accessible and clearly labelled (and, of course, properly marked)?
- Are all pupils represented in the work on display?
- Are class and individual targets easy to find?

Resources and useful further reading

www.education.gov.uk/everychildmatters (Every Child Matters) – even for the current government, this still contains important ideas.

www.nationalcollege.org.uk

www.ofsted.gov.uk (Ofsted Framework and Evaluation Schedule) – it is very important that you are aware of this.

The Children Act 2004 http://www.legislation.gov.uk/ukpga/2004/31/contents

Creating Effective Networks

Caroline Dargan

In this chapter, we will consider the following:

- Networking – what do we mean?
- Possible concerns about the way networkers are perceived
- The purpose of networks
- So what's next – putting it into practice?
- A good networker's skills and attributes
- Educational networks

Web 2.0 has changed the capacity for information and learning opportunities outside formal education settings (blogs and wikis). There is also a profusion of forums and informational directories so networking is alive and well. In this chapter, therefore, let's see what we already know about building a professional network and how we could use networking as a resource tool for all, enabling connectors to share skills, attitudes and knowledge.

Networking – what do we mean?

Networks are:

- about making connections for general or specific purposes for a group or group of individuals
- groups of connectors with linked foci and purpose
- about deepening the quality of interactions of fellow professionals by sharing tools and techniques
- used for supporting professional development and as a resource tool to help groups reach a common goal

- authentic to the chosen set of values and beliefs, while growing mutually beneficial relationships that assist people in reaching goals
- about providing information to help people make the important decisions needed to improve professional practices.

Networking:

- can provide an objective sounding board to help solve ongoing dilemmas or issues and allows you to connect work with others to find common solutions
- allows space and legitimacy for the sharing of information, experiences, ideas and solutions
- is an inclusive activity that thrives best when combined with imaginative diversity and free thinking
- is about gaining leverage by building effective relationships with other professionals in the profession
- is about building a mutually beneficial group that sets and achieves chosen goals.

Networking is all about connections

Networking needs to be a strong focus, in all correspondence, conversations and connections that the group/individuals are involved in, in order to:

- be linked with others with similar thinking
- consort or keep company with those we are linked to
- link up with correspondence (written or online).

Possible concerns about the way networkers are perceived

Networking can be perceived as off-putting if you feel uncomfortable in social situations you are not in control of. The 20th-century version of net-workers and networking was detached and manipulative. This was a misnomer for professional networking but the perception still existed because of publi-cised information relating to some shallow self-orientated and manipulative behaviours that were highlighted in the business world, with images such as 'greed is good' in the *Wall Street* movie, the portrayed 'no such thing as society' political belief and 1980s' phenomena such as avarice and greed within the yuppie community. These still live on in some people's minds.

So we need to put networking in its true place in professional life. In this forum, networking is about a genuine belief and interest in linking with other professionals, inputting and assisting understanding wherever possible. But regardless of sector, private or public, when the networker's input is real and transparent, it will lead to purposeful relationships and stimulating interactions.

The power of effecting networks is about building worthwhile relationships and maximising opportunities. The intention behind networking is crucial if there is to be clarity around the manipulation issue. If the intent of the network has a strong moral purpose, such as improving learning experience and environments for all, this reduces opportunities for the group to be manipulative, shallow or self-orientated.

Networking in education or health, for example, is about influencing others to work towards the greater good because if we are all fit, healthy and literate and numerate, it benefits all members of society. Networks will not grow or sustain themselves unless there is trust, value and benefit for all, as the basis of that network. Of course, individuals and groups can abuse networks but, as said, if the core purpose and overall intent is authentically based on learning, there is less likelihood of manipulative or negative behaviours.

We do not have to accept the negative premise for networking in the groups we set up or join. We can overcome this by setting up the core ethos of our networking philosophy. If we have been authentic in our setting up of the goals and objectives of the networking group, and grounded them in moral imperatives of true educators, we can feel safe that will flourish as their base. Networks can easily function as positive, humble, generous and purposeful.

The purpose of networks

So why do people–organisations start or join networks?

- Building ways of meeting new people
- Building new learning platforms
- Building new knowledge forums
- Building new solutions to old dilemmas
- Building a sharing community for the greater good

What are the benefits of building a local, national or international network?

- Resource pool
- Support pool
- Performance pool
- Knowledge pool

We can use acronyms to show the core purpose of the group and what it wants from the network, which helps others know who the group are. For example:

Negotiating – ways of conversing, influencing and persuading

Engagement – encouraging connectors and relating through parallel contexts, values, ethos and core purpose

Talking – discussions, debating and dialogues as part of the process to set common goals and outcomes

Working with – individual and group interactions to develop a synergy that persuades networks to move forward towards their desired outcomes

Organising – setting up foci and/or direction(s) for the group that proactively develops situations and events to enhance the group

Relationships – building rapport, trust in communities, groups and individuals, enhancing mutually beneficial attitudes and events

Knowledge – new learning platforms, research, leading-edge practices and latest information that has an advantage for everyone in the fast-changing pace of 21st-century life

Supportive – a place for taking risks, sharing and challenging their own and others' learning

Networking as a natural link to the connective theory of human relationships – six degrees of separation

Networking has gained from the idea of the six degrees of separation theory which came from Frigyes Karnthy's short story, *Chains*, published in 1929. The theory is that anyone can be connected with another through a chain of acquaintances that has no more than five intermediaries. In 2001, Duncan Watts of Columbia University continued research into the phenomenon and recreated the theory using the internet. He used an email message as the focus that needed to be delivered. After reviewing the data collected by 48,000 senders, 19 targets and 157 countries, Watts found the average number of intermediaries was just six, as it was in Karnthy's original research. Your network group can use ideas such as the six degrees of separation concept to build a network.

So what's next – putting it into practice?

Whether you want to join a group or set up your own network, you will want to ask yourselves various questions. You will also need to identify and structure your networking goals.

Questions for reflection

- Should we set up our group and, if we do, how will we do that?
- If not, how will joining a group enable our organisation to flourish?
- If you are joining a group, you may wish to think through the questions below:

  o Who were the founders?
  o Who are the organisers?
  o How is the base group structured?

○ What's their influence?
○ What's the group success and ethos?

- What will be the overt benefits for you/the group?
- What time-resource input would you/the group need to allow?

Starting to network

What do we need to know before we start?

Your organisation needs to understand who the most productive contacts to touch base with are. It is an uncomfortable truth that not everyone you link up with will be able to network or be of value as a networker; this, of course, is not to say that the non-targeted individuals are not valuable as people, nor is it meant as a criticism of them. This is why setting up a criteria assessment is helpful and needs to be devised; then your organisation can assess who the most productive groups/individuals to pinpoint are. When starting to network, there will be the need to develop a process that helps you build a structural matrix, for example it could be a simple three-tiered matrix, like the one below:

Yes group – people linked to similar goal foci, likely to want to participate, be placed to help, a referrer, stakeholder or linker

Maybe group – people you enjoy meeting and who have the energy to link in but are at present unlikely to fulfil the criteria in the yes group

Unlikely group – people or groups who are unable to connect in a way that encourages networking principles or who are unable to grow networking opportunities.

Questions for reflection

- Is everyone in the focus team for the organisation on board?
- Encourage/brainstorm their connectors to form a database for your group (see the network diagram).
- Agree a common networking process.
- Set a team time to focus on networking creativity and feed back on what's happening (e.g. once every three months).
- Use the intranet to update the networking contacts database and input by contacts.
- Are there more questions at this stage?
- Why are we focusing on networking at this time and what do we want from it?
- Where are we on the concept of networking?
- What's our next first step?
- How will we focus on this alongside all the other initiatives and targets in the organisation's schedule?

Setting networking goals for your team

Start networking with a purpose by asking these questions:

- What are we trying to achieve and how will networking enhance that?
- Who do we need to link in to and why? (Brainstorm possibilities)
- How will we recognise our outcomes and their impact (measurement, return on investment)?

Designing and constructing a networking plan

- Set up and state the networking goals and aims.
- Develop a strategy and step-by-step process on how the team will work towards the goals.
- Design a success criteria format from the YES list and state how you will meet them and stay in touch with them.
- Perform a criteria assessment of the networking 'assets'.

Goal setting as part of the networking process

Goal setting is a very powerful technique and enhances the networking process. The process of setting goals and targets allows you to choose what you have in the structure. By knowing precisely what you need to achieve, it's then easier to concentrate on something and improve it. Goal setting gives a long–term vision and short–term motivation. It helps keep the focus on the acquisition of knowledge skills and helps to organise the assets. By setting transparent and distinct goals, the milestones can be measured and success celebrated.

Setting goals means you can:

- achieve more;
- improve behavioural performance;
- increase your motivation to achieve;
- increase your gratification and satisfaction in the achievements.

Setting goals effectively

The way in which you set networking goals strongly affects their likelihood of being achieved.

- Passionate yet realistic statement: express your goals decidedly.
- Focus: if you set an exact goal with outcomes, the achievement can be measured.
- Set priorities and strategies: 80 per cent focus brings an 80 per cent result.
- Write out the goals, as research suggests this helps to achieve them (there is a 50 per cent improvement in comparison to just verbalising them).
- Daily strategies need to be small and achievable (example: how do you eat an elephant? Answer: a bit at a time).

An interesting idea – goals not targets

A group may want to set behavioural goals for their network, along with strategies of how to change before setting other outcome goals. 'What got you here won't get you there' (Goldsmith, 2008). This then means your group has control of the situation. The group then keeps the network true to the initial ethical concept.

If the original goals are behavioural, skills or knowledge based, then you can keep control over the achievement of your goals. For example, if we take education as the group, the network group can focus on the goal to improving teaching and learning; children do not reach national standards, but there was better than expected improvement in all learners' progress, therefore the goal was achieved and there was success to celebrate. This is then a highly motivating factor in continuing with the networking group that supported and challenged the goals set by the group.

The networking concept works well on many levels

Networks fit perfectly with the technology-based era, which means they engage all generations from baby boomers to millenniums.

Networks also build on all the research about focusing on effective adult learning environments. Adults learn through their experience: adults see the world as they are, not as it is. Using coaching questions helps people understand that there are many ways to see the world and that their way is just one way of seeing it. A coaching curiosity when interacting encourages connectors to build effective rapport with others.

Adults learn from modelled behaviours: good practice is often learnt by seeing other people do things well or less effectively. Overt and focused modelling of good practice helps others' understanding of the impact of their skills and behaviours.

Adults prefer bespoke support: special relationships and networks can be developed through using coaching questions based on curiosity, which helps others think about their key challenges.

In leading our peers, effective interactions with others who are objective gives people a core structure, which can build self-confidence, self-esteem and motivation. This helps people move towards their goals and potential. So if we build environments that respect adults as learners and further develop technology as a gateway, how do we set our networking ethos and principles out for all to see?

A good networker's skills and attributes

1 **Communication in all forms** is one of the most dynamic talents of a successful networker. Communication in its truest form is not just about talking; in fact, it can be the opposite. Real and effective communication is as much

about listening, valuing, building a relationship and adding to others' experiences. Research like that of Mehrabian (1971) suggests that words only have a 7 per cent impact in communications when people are under pressure. The more one listens, the greater the impact it can have on others. Listening is an active process not a passive one. Active listening ensures reflection, reflecting back or paraphrasing what's been said so that the listener is reassured that they have communicated what they intended to. In networking, it is incredibly important to listen well. Ask yourself what is your normal ratio of listening and talking in your interactions; if you tend to talk-advise more than listen, you will need to switch your focus in networking situations. A focused listener benefits by gaining information, enabling others to become better networkers and offers future subsequent chances for next steps.

2 **A good networker can express themselves in person or through technology.** Networkers need to be able to express what they want, believe and are passionate about; in this way they can engage and influence others. Often it is helpful to develop a 60-second blurb for your introduction, or a hook to engage others. By using this tool, you can learn not to just make plain statements and this can bring your role to life. The more elaborate statement gives the listener licence to elaborate in their blurb. The secret to stimulating networking conversations is to add connecting information, so that others can banter with you. Good connectors test out their views and thoughts, probe through questioning that generates attention on the key topics and ponder on the comments or responses. This way, the connector gets a concrete feel for what is important and how they can move the group/individual forward. Then the connector can expect reciprocal behaviours from other connectors. The richer the involvement of conversational dialogue, the greater the gains and interest from the listener.

3 **A good networker sees networking as an important tool.** Other people can often pick up signs of disinterest or false engagement. It is insulting to others if they believe you do not take a real interest in the process. So the reverse will hold true too: your passion and stories of your networking experiences and input will shine through. Showing the benefits and values the network offers to you for others to hear, is an excellent way of showing your belief in the process.

Good networkers behave in a way that is genuine and it means others are not mistrustful of unsavoury motives. They do not keep out of debates as they know sharing with others is the fairest approach in networking; your input could be the element others need to engage.

4 **A good networker is a curious questioner.** Curiosity is a strong driver as it means the networker's questioning stays away from interrogation or just the finding out of information. Networkers like others to be interested and by asking appropriate questions you can show curiosity and motivate the speaker to say more. Questions encourage others to link in with each other emotionally and professionally. Questioning done slowly and focused on the speaker can release pressure and give people an opportunity to express big issues. Questioning can help others focus on important events and points of interest. Are you well practiced and up to date on questioning techniques?

5 **A good networker is an active listener.** All adults enjoy having others listen to them, in a non-threatening environment, as they express their views and ideas. In networking, the asking of significant questions is reliant on active listening; people will feel flattered and the questioning gives them a sign that the listener respects the speaker. Learning to listen and not waiting to talk is very hard for many people but is an absolute must for an effective networker. The idea of practicing active listening is perhaps rather unusual but we are all sometimes pretend, self-centred or limited listeners. This has to be practiced for most of us not to fall into any of those categories. Being conscious about your responsibility as a listener is not something you can fake for very long. Even if others do not know consciously, they will 'sense' you have tuned out, and this is not the most effective way to build rapport and trust. The perfect listener is always in 'the here and now'.

6 **A good networker uses emotional intelligence in relationship management.** This is the most important part of relationship development; if you do not understand your own blockers and triggers, you will find it exceptionally difficult to manage your relationships with others. If you are in denial of your own needs and desires in a relationship, you will find it hard to have an independent and effective networking relationship.

Effective networkers never get into a destructive disagreement cycle as it is not productive; they are happy to disagree but stop at trying to prove they are right at the expense of others. If they feel they need to address a situation which means criticizing another, they will address the negatives they perceive will harm the group rather than attack an individual.

A self-assessment questionnaire would be helpful to assess where you are now. Why not take the test and then look at your areas for development. Is it the same for others in your group? What can you improve and how will you do that – make a plan? Then what?

Table 13.1

Self-assessment	Yes	OK	Uneasy
I am confident in unknown situations			
I can make a cold call to contact others			
At events I can work a room to build contacts			
I am good at remembering details about others I meet			
I am good at asking for support			
I share resources, information and support with others			
I have lots of pastimes and belong to various groups and communities			
I keep my contact list live with planned events and meetings			
I use technology to enhance my network professionally			
I cope with negativity or conflict effectively			

Understanding the importance of building rapport and trust

'The most important single ingredient in the formula of success is knowing how to get along with people' (Theodore Roosevelt). Absolutely! He is talking about rapport, which is a feeling of being on the same wavelength as another person, the ability to appreciate one another's feelings and understand someone else's viewpoint. Many people see the ability to develop rapport as the key to influencing others. Here are three concepts for developing rapport and trust:

- **Focused purpose** – this empowers the group to start building on similar experiences, traits, ideas, interests, or values that they have in common. This is a powerful way of developing the networking process. Identifying focused purpose comes from drawing people out with questions and sharing self with others.
- **Associations** – once networkers have identified their common strands, a symbiotic bond naturally develops. This association can lead to greater empathy and stronger communication. These threads and associations allow networkers to be part of the start of a radical evolution, which enables them to be free to exchange ideas, innovate and work together toward common goals.
- **Partnership** – this is the heart of good networking, and building a solid base by developing rapport is the cornerstone of the relationship. Seeking those with focused strands in order to make associations starts with well-honed communication skills and ends in networking partnerships. This type of networking offers a thrilling platform for professional dialogue and development in education.

Educational networks

Networking meetings can be:

- social
- strategic
- leading
- practical.

The audience can consist of:

- support staff
- teachers
- middle leaders
- senior leaders

- deputy heads
- head teachers.

Possible objectives include:

- solution seeking
- a resource bank
- an information update
- research development
- career opportunities.

Relevance to role:

- classroom support
- classroom practices
- subject practices
- SENCO
- phase leaders
- curriculum leaders
- directors of Faculties
- assistant heads – new, next steps
- deputies – new to role, career, ready for headship
- heads – new, experienced system leaders.

Benefits of educational networking:

- improves children's life chances
- develops professional roles to meet current demands
- improves CPD and higher attaining professional standards
- informs the up-skilling, upgrading and informational process
- becomes part of the coaching and mentoring feedback programme
- allows for resource, skill and good practice sharing
- provides modelling, shadowing opportunities
- encourages motivational sharing and contribution to debates, discussion and dialogues
- leads to publishing and research opportunities.

Functions of networking

The functions of networking can be envisioned in many different ways and developed totally by the group. Here are some examples:

Influencing national and local policies through a professional network rather than the more traditional routes would provide a network that could be apolitical, similar to the medical or legal professions.

Discussing with diverse and assorted teachers from many different schools can provide insights into understanding government policies and consequences. It can bring forward possibilities for rethinking or restructuring initiatives.

Localizing groups would be able to share professional practice, in teaching, learning or leading, again through different or more diverse routes than were available in the 20th century and the first decade of the 21st century.

Initiative development by professionals can be the core principle that the groups offer to creators or innovators of new practices that are working in situ alongside universities or researchers.

So what's next?

Are ideas and practices that were seen as unworkable in the past now possible using technology?

How can the group discover the local expertise in the network and engage those who are not on board, offering benefits and value to the non-engagers?

What assumptions is the network making about adult learning? (Andragogy)

Networking in a learning world

A network can be an influential approach to baseline school improvement. Research in the USA and Holland suggests that specific networks have encouraged schools to shape their own curriculum development. This has grown in the second decade of the 21st century, especially with the emergence of less government input–control. The network can support and challenge the pedagogical, analogical and methodological approaches which can open up all possibilities for the profession to take the lead in improvements in learning and teaching practices, giving back authority and status to professional-led developments (or practitioners in any field).

Proprietorship of the network

This depends on the formal or informal basis of the network (perhaps with an instrument of practice?). Important components of this are:

- dispersed ownership within a framework, no domination
- a format that is flexible but has a core structure
- focusing on the participant's needs, wishes, and desires
- accepting the challenge format as a driver of the network
- being sustainable for all groups within the network.

These aspects are important facets when thinking about how you get started in setting up a group or joining a group, especially if you already have an organisation.

Unlimited professionalism

Networks based on professional sharing are about moving schools into future thinking, on curriculum, effective classroom practice, management and leadership development. Understanding research and cutting-edge knowledge in a specific area helps move the profession forward. The critical friend model used in many networking groups helps professionals see observations, assessments and reviews as an entitlement of development rather than an intrusion of officialdom and external agency practices. Then the professionals become critical, reflective practitioners with a challenging yet support audience of like-minded equals. The network can give the professionals a shared and powerful voice which can enhance the education development within that network. This is especially helpful in difficult economic times.

Conclusion

The 21st century is one of verbalisation and articulation, sharing skills, talents and information through the internet and face to face. Networking can be the process that places connectors at the forefront of professional innovation. Networking is the perfect forum for forward-thinking connectors who interact through colligate participation in worldwide networks. I hope this chapter has inspired you to get connected!

Questions for further thinking

- What skills do you need to develop?
- What information and knowledge do you need?
- What help, assistance or association do you need?
- If you start or join a network, what will it look/feel like?
- Are your goals for being in the network sustainable?
- Will the network be local, national or international?
- What can block your progress?
- How do you include your stakeholders and get them on board with the networking process?
- Is there a better way of moving forward?
- Who are you not asking?

There are no case studies in this chapter but there have been professional conversations with head teachers, various professionals and business leaders. The names are given below and I thank them greatly for their contributions to the thinking and ideas put forward in this chapter.

Discussions with colleagues on networking and networks

Ms S Birch Woodcock, primary head teacher, London
Mr M Crowe, coaching director, TFK, London
Ms R Leeke, secondary head teacher, London
Ms F Morris, Future Leader assistant head, London
Mr H Ravel, business consultant, London
Jenny Palmer, Southampton
Duncan Garbett, Staffordshire
Gillian Doxzon, California
Maggy Ames, New York City
Rosalind Edgar, Australia

Resources and useful further reading

Cisco Networking Academy is a global education program that teaches students how to design, build, troubleshoot, and secure computer networks for increased access to career and economic opportunities in communities around the world. http://www.cisco.com/web/learning/netacad/index.html

Cordingley, A. et al. (2003) Impact of Collaborative CPD on Classroom Teaching and Learning. London: IoE: SSRU EPPI-Centre.

D'Souza, D. (2008) Brilliant Networking. Harlow: Pearson.

Fisher, D. and Vilas, S. (2000) Power Networking, 2nd edition. London: Bard Press.

Gdudaris.com – networking with a purpose and a plan.

Goldsmith, M. (2008) What Got You Here Won't Get You There. London: Profile Books.

Karinthy, F. (1929) Chains – a short story which creates the notion of 6 degrees of separation. In Minden maskpennen van (Hungary), now out of print.

Knowles, M., Goddard, E. and Speck, E. (2003) Adult Learning documents (1985–2003). Available at: www.jinedupnetworking.com – some excellent guidelines.

Lieberman, A. and Grolnick, M. (1996) Networks and Reform in American Education. Teacher College Record, 98(1): 7–45.

LinkedIn – a professional networking site www.linkedin.com

Mehrabian, A. (1971) Silent Messages. Belmont, CA: Wadsworth.

Olson, J. et al. (2010) Changing the Subject: the Challenge to Teacher Professionalism in OECD Countries. Journal of Curriculum Studies, 31(1): 69–82.

Timperley, J. (2002) Network Your Way to Success. London: Piatkus Books.

Youtube – video for education networking: there are a number of excellent examples on this site www.youtube.com

Index

Acland Burghley School, 152–152
action planning, 7, 27–29
action research, 161–163
   action research methodologies,
      166–168
   action research project, 170–171

benchmarking, 88–89
budgets, 81–84

Camden Secondary Learning Support Service,
   154–157
career development, 68–70
Centre for Monitoring and Evaluating,
   103
Chelsea Academy, 111–112
change
   gaining buy-in, 132–134
   identification of need for, 129–132
   leading/managing, 25, 67, 138–139
   models of 127–129
coaching and mentoring, 12–15, 57–59
   National Framework for, 13
co-construction of learning, 116
conflict
   analysing, 39–40
   causes of, 34–35
   managing, 27
culture, 4, 5–6, 25–26, 148
curriculum planning, 119, 147

data
   analysing, 104–105
   base levels, 98
   numerical assessment data, 98
   types of, 96–97
   using data for analysis, 98–101
distributed leadership, 63–64, 146
Doha College, Qatar, 6–7

emotional intelligence, 4, 27, 35, 135
Every Child Matters, 19, 185–186

expenditure
   monitoring, 85
   patterns of, 87
   reporting progress on, 86–87

Fischer Family Trust, 103
funding, 80–81

goal setting, 194–195
Gregorc, thinking styles, 37–39

Hampstead Secondary School, 149
healthy schools, 20, 26
holding to account, 10, 41–42

inclusion, definitions, 142–144
improvement planning 84, 130– 132, 137–138
inspection
   during inspection, 182–185
   pre inspection, 179–182

John Donne Primary School, 145–147

Key Stage 3 curriculum, 112–116
Key Stage 4 curriculum, 118–123
Kolb's model of learning and
     development, 72–73

leadership styles, 11–12
leading and managing, 6, 62, 154
   change 138 –9
   in inclusive education, 144
   professional learning and development, 48
   and wellbeing, 19, 21, 23
learning community, 49–50
Listen Ear Project, 149–151

Maslow's Hierarchy of Need, 72, 154–156
mission statement, 7–8
motivation, 35–37
   Motivational Maps, 36–37
   Herzberg, theory of, 72

National Occupational Standards, 74
networking, 189–190
  and collaboration, 58
  purpose, 191
  starting, 193
  skills, 196–197

Ofsted, 175–177
  framework, 19, 177–179

performance management, 50
professional development, 3, 8–10, 44–47,
    53–54, 123–124, 148
  leading, 48–50
  nine factors, 54–55

RAISEonline, 102–1 03
resilience, 31

self-efficacy 20–21
self-evaluation, 163–165, 168–170
self-knowledge, 4–5

six degrees of separation, 192
stress, 18–19
support staff, 64–66
  and action research,165

Transactional Analysis, 70–71
trust, 3–5, 25–26, 198

value added, 101–102
  contextual value added, 102
values, 4–5, 143
value for money, 88
vision, 6–8, 135–136, 144

wellbeing
  and inclusion, 148
  definitions 17–18
  national and international policies,
    18–20
  planning for 21–22
well-being programme, 27–29
work–life balance, 23

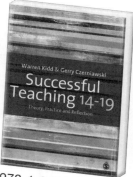